NATIVE GEMS
For His Crown

Gary Klumpenhower

Native Gems for His Crown

ISBN: 978-0-9792739-2-6
Printed in the United States of America
©2007 by Gary Klumpenhower

Interior photography by Gary Klumpenhower
Cover and interior design by Isaac Publishing, Inc.

Isaac Publishing, Inc.
P.O. 342
Three Rivers, MI 49093
www.isaacpublishing.com

No part of this book may be reproduced or transmitted in any form or by any means, electronic or mechanical—including photocopying, recording, or by any information storage and retrieval system—without permission in writing from the publisher. Please direct your inquires to admin@isaacpublishing.com

ACKNOWLEDGMENTS

I wish to acknowledge the wonderful assistance I have received in putting this book together from my wife, Helen, and from our four sons, Jack, David, Jim, and Mark and their wives. Mark and his wife, Sharon, have done most of the editing work. Also, the suggestions and ideas from Sherry Gilmore and Pam Eichorn of Isaac Publishing, Inc., are much appreciated and have been very helpful.

Jewels (When He Cometh)

Words by William O. Cushing
Music by George F. Root

Verse 1
When He cometh, when He cometh
To make up His jewels,
All His jewels, precious jewels,
His loved and His own.

Chorus:
Like the stars of the morning, His bright crown adorning,
They shall shine in their beauty, Bright gems for His crown.

Verse 2
He will gather, He will gather
The gems for His kingdom;
All the pure ones, all the bright ones,
His loved and His own.

Verse 3
Little children, little children,
Who love their Redeemer,
Are the jewels, precious jewels,
His loved and His own.

©1967 Copyright by Tabernacle Publishing Co. Chicago, Illinois 60644
"Favorite Hymns of Praise"

CONTENTS

Foreword
Preface: Trust and Obey
Acknowledgments

Chapter One:
The Calling 1
The Way West
The Land I Will Show You

Chapter Two
Utah 9
Brigham City
Digging In
Heart Trouble
Salt Lake City
Come Over and Help Us

Chapter Three
Toadlena 35
Moving In
A Community in Poverty
The Middle of Nowhere
Reaching the Lost
A Raw Environment
Camp Work
Worship and Outreach
The Expansion of the Gospel Message
Bringers of Another Gospel
Newcomb
Life as a Missionary Family
Changing Times
Difficulties from Within
A Roaring Lion
Toward the End of Our Toadlena Tenure
Farewells

Chapter Four
Tohatchi 101
First Navajo Christian Reformed Church
The Work Begins
School Town
A Growing Church
Try Bingo
Satan's Snares
In Times of Need
The Next Generation
Gems
Fun and Relaxation
Wellandport
Moving On

Chapter Five
Window Rock 155
A New Landscape
An Immediate Concern
The Window Rock Congregation
Surgery Once More
Oppositions
New Members
Different Work
Volunteer Helpers
Preparing for the Years Ahead

Conclusion 187
Epilogue 193

FOREWARD

By Jack Klumpenhower

I arrived on the Navajo reservation in January of 1969, in the back seat of the family car. I was five, just old enough to look out the car window and understand that life would be different from the city I was used to. There were fewer houses and more sand, and it took a long time to get anywhere. I was told Dad would have a new job as pastor of a church. We would live in a different house. And I would ride a school bus to get to kindergarten.

So it was that a few weeks later the school bus pulled up to the parking area at our new church, below our new house. It was snowing. Mom put me in rubber, buckle-down snow boots and gave me my shoes to carry. The boots were common enough where we'd come from, but unknown and decidedly dorky-looking on the reservation. I took the big step up into the bus filled with strangers, slipped on some ice and fell on my face in front of the driver. The shoes went tumbling down the aisle.

Looking back on it now, I see how clearly my family was ill-suited for the work on the reservation. We were misfits. But God uses clumsy and imperfect people. Over the next 33 years, he would use us and many others for Jesus. Dad was faithful to the call to ministry, and God did the work. I don't fully understand it, but I know that those years of imperfect ministry will fit God's plan. Perfectly.

Dad has titled this book after a hymn that is, in turn, based on an Old Testament passage from Zechariah. The prophet envisioned a coming king who was powerful enough to rule the world but also humble enough to ride a donkey:

> "He will proclaim peace to the nations.
> His rule will extend from sea to sea.
> The LORD their God will serve them on that day
> as the flock of his people.
> They will sparkle in his land
> like jewels in a crown." (Zechariah 9:10, 16, NIV)

Jesus, of course, quietly proclaimed himself to be that king when he rode an untrained donkey into Jerusalem. Followers of Jesus are like their king. We don't ride gallantly into ministry on a noble horse. Our arrival is more donkey-like. But lumbering as we were, my family was privileged to be witnesses as Jesus extended his kingdom across seas and deserts to Navajoland.

Dad is retired now. Once again, he has faithfully answered the call to testify to God's goodness—this time by writing this book. He has struggled. English is not his first language, and many of the sentences are awkward, the stories uneven, the words clumsy. Dad has asked for help, and some of my brothers have stepped in as editors. Their skillful work has greatly improved this book and has been an outstanding service to Dad.

But I have resisted. Although I am now a professional writer, I have offered no comments nor changed a single sentence. I don't want to make this book better. It is Dad's story about God's work, and it is perfect as it is.

Jack Klumpenhower
Durango, Colorado

PREFACE

TRUST AND OBEY

Abraham is one of my favorite Bible characters. Throughout my lifetime I have often thought of him and of the various experiences he had to face in life. Although he was a faithful man of God, life certainly was not always easy for him. This was the case in spite of the fact that the Lord had given His promise to bless him. God's people must grow and mature in their relationship with the Lord if they expect the Lord to use them in His kingdom. The best soldiers are the battle-hardened soldiers.

Abraham was told by God to leave his homeland and his relatives and friends and go to a land that the Lord would show him. If he obeyed and put his trust in the Lord, God would surely bless him. We are told that Abraham left and did as he was told. The Bible says that he did this because of his faith in God—and God's people are able to accomplish great things if they have true faith in God that is demonstrated in a knowledge of Him, as well as a full confidence in Him.

Abraham arrived in the land of Canaan, the place where God wanted him to be. The Canaanites, who had already established themselves there, would be potential troublemakers and enemies. The land was also notorious for times of drought, making this new land an uncertain place to build a future upon. Certainly it must not have seemed like much of a blessing from the Lord to a rancher and livestock raiser like Abraham. God had placed him in the middle of a dangerous, sinful, and needy land. Life in Canaan would not be a bed of roses. Still, Abraham continued to follow the Lord and serve Him, even though the Lord was incomprehensible to him.

Wherever he went, he built an altar to the Lord where he could spend time in worship. He learned to be content with whatever the Lord had in mind for him. This is why we are told that he was willing to live in tents, so he could move from place to place in search of more food for his cattle. In the meantime, we are also told that he kept looking ahead to "the city with foundations whose architect and builder is God." (Hebrews 11:10). Each morning, when he picked himself up off the floor in his tent, he must have reminded himself of eternal glory that he would receive some day. Abraham must have gained strength from looking forward to his eternal reward. Ultimately, Abraham would not only survive in Canaan, but thrive there as well.

My wife, Helen, and I were called by God to a life of ministry to the Navajo people in Utah, New Mexico, and Arizona. As with Abraham, it was not an easy assignment, but a good one. At times, we had to experience problems and battles and disappointments that we were not prepared for in advance. But our faithful God was always there blessing us. Never have we had a sense of self-pity as a result of living a long distance from friends and relatives. The Lord blessed us with many new friends and brothers and sisters in Christ. We feel deeply honored by the Lord to have been involved in bringing the message of salvation to the Navajo people for forty years.

Often people have said to me, "You should write a book about your work and experiences." Now, in my retirement, I finally decided to do so. I have relied heavily upon input from my wife, Helen, who is blessed with a wonderful memory. The Lord has helped us to recall many of the experiences we had and lessons we learned that may be beneficial if shared with others.

This book was put together for the sake of our Navajo readers, as well as all others. Hopefully this will serve as a reminder of how the Lord is building His kingdom also among the Native American people of North America. Often, during one of the countless children's Bible school classes and VBS's, we would sing an old children's hymn with the chorus:

> *Like the stars of the morning,*
> *His bright crown adorning,*
> *They will shine in their beauty,*
> *Bright gems for His crown.*

The Navajo believers are the native "gems for His crown." They deserve and need our love and support and may not be forgotten, as the Lord has surely not forgotten them.

CHAPTER 1

The Calling

THE WAY WEST

It was Monday, July 8, 1963. By nine o'clock that morning, the North American moving van had already pulled up in front of our house at 1011½ Sherman Street in Grand Rapids, Michigan. The movers had come to pick up our meager belongings. We were ready as most of our belongings had been packed in boxes by us in advance. It did not take long to empty our apartment. Most young, student families were not known to have a lot of earthly possessions and we were certainly no exception to that. By noon, the apartment was empty and we even managed to give it a final cleaning.

We had lived there for the first eleven months of our married life. It had been a time of finishing up school and hoping and praying that the Lord would put us to work somewhere in his kingdom. Back in 1898, the Board of Missions of the Christian Reformed Church, or CRC, had sent its first missionaries to work with the Navajo Indians of the American Southwest. Today we were setting out for our first assignment in Brigham City, Utah to work with the Navajo. Although our plan was to leave during the middle of the afternoon, we were too excited to wait. Earlier that morning I had taken our two-month old son Jack to his Aunt Alice who had kindly agreed to watch him. We had lunch there as planned, but could wait no longer. We said our good-byes, and then the three of us—myself, Helen, and Jack—set off for the American Southwest.

Earlier that year we had purchased a 1957 Ford Fairlane. It was in such fine condition that it seemed almost too good for a student family, but it proved to be just what we needed and served us well for several years. We had plenty of room for our luggage and a few other personal items. Jack traveled on the back seat in a

Chapter One: The Calling

strong cardboard box with a newly purchased mattress to keep him comfortable. This would serve as his car seat as well as bassinet during the trip. The joke, naturally, was that we took along a true Jack-in-the-Box.

We traveled south to Kalamazoo and from there towards the Chicago area where we would be arriving around rush hour. The heavy traffic there was a serious concern as neither of us was familiar with that part of the country. In order to avoid some of the traffic, we decided to go south at Portage, Indiana and hook up with U.S. Highway 30. For the next four days, this road would take us across the country all the way to our new home in Utah. As there was not yet a freeway system, we would be forced to drive a two-lane highway through the heart of America. U.S. Highway 30 also went through the center of many cities. On this day, we still had to go through downtown Joliet, Illinois.

Finally we reached open country and began to breathe easier. As we got up to 55 miles per hour, we could see the open farmland of Illinois. It was a beautiful sight. I had traveled through the "breadbasket" of America once before and was aware of the wonderful crops on that fertile soil. The large fields of corn and soybeans impressed me once again. In my heart I wished my father would some day be able to see this land.

Both Helen and I grew up in farming families. My parents had both been born in the Netherlands, and had raised a family of seven children there. We underwent tough times during the German invasion and occupation during World War II. My father had even spent some time as a prisoner of war, and my mother had to raise her young family for much of the war by herself. We all immigrated to Canada in 1950 when I was 12 years old, and since then had struggled to make ends meet. At this time they were on a farm near Rockwood, Ontario which was too small for them all to get by on. It was a family that, like Abraham, had been tested by fire and had found strong faith and favor with God.

Helen had been raised on a vegetable farm—this one in Eastern Michigan near a town called Imlay City. Her father lost a farm in the Great Depression, but later managed to buy another one. After elementary school, Helen had been temporarily unable

Chapter One: The Calling

to continue her education because her mother was ill. As the oldest of the four daughters, she was expected to stay at home and help her mother with housework. By 1963, both of her parents had died from cancer.

These tough experiences had given us two things that we both shared. We had learned at an early age to trust in the Lord's providence. We had also learned to do without many luxuries. These were lessons that would certainly come in handy in our upcoming years in the mission field.

Towards late evening, the sun went down and the sky ahead turned a beautiful red. It was the promise of good traveling weather—and hopefully other good things—ahead. We trusted that He who holds the future would also hold our hand. It was dark by the time we crossed the Mississippi River into the town of Clinton, Iowa, where we spent our first night. After a good meal, we had no trouble falling asleep.

That next morning we breakfasted on sandwiches in the motel. We had to be careful with our money. The Mission Board had given us enough to cover our traveling expenses, but we were aware that this would also have to carry us until our first paycheck came a month later.

As we traveled west through Iowa and into Nebraska, Helen, who knew her U.S. history, reflected on the fact that we were certainly not the first people to come this way before with thoughts of starting a new life in the West. We were now traveling along the Platte River, where over 125 years earlier the first white pioneers had blazed a trail to Oregon that would be followed by thousands more over the next decade. This was also the route of the old Mormon Trail, as they were pushed out of Illinois and moved into Utah back in the 1840's.

This was certainly not the life I had planned on as a boy. Even after immigration to Canada I had dreams of one day becoming a chicken farmer. But then, one night, when I was twelve years old and still a recent immigrant, a new dream came to me vividly in the night. I was sure that someone had said to me in an audible voice, "Gary, I want you to become a minister." It startled me and I was shaking all over. The idea of becoming a minister had

3

Chapter One: The Calling

never before entered my mind. I woke up my parents and said to them, "I think that I have to become a minister." It took a while for my father to wake up, but with my mother's urging he did. He sat up and said, "What were you saying?" I repeated my story. After a quiet moment he said to me, "If this is what the Lord wants from you, then this is a good thing and we shall do everything possible to help you." My mother agreed, and she assured me that we would talk more about this the following day.

I learned from my mother that as a young girl she had a deep desire to go into mission work herself. However, this had been impossible. As one of twelve children in a working-class family, she had to leave home at age 13 to work for a farmer to earn her own room and board. School beyond the elementary grades was for the most part unavailable to working-class people. Additionally, many people in the Netherlands believed that schooling for girls, who would become mothers and homemakers, was quite unnecessary. Perhaps now the Lord had in mind to use her children in the mission field instead of her.

My mother reminded me that, if I was to become a minister, I would have to go to school for many years. I did not enjoy school, and the whole idea of having to attend it for many more years had never entered my mind. Furthermore, I was already looking forward to getting work somewhere to help our immigrant family make ends meet by bringing home a few extra dollars every week. All throughout high school and on into college, I would have gladly walked away and quit had it not been for that night when I heard that voice.

Helen also had been led by the Lord as I had been. Even though her high school had been delayed, her parents had the wisdom to understand her desire. Arrangements were made for her to attend Ferris Institute in Big Rapids, Michigan, where she would receive her high school diploma. Later she attended college and earned her BA degree and a teaching certificate. She then taught in Christian elementary schools for three years in Hudsonville and Grand Rapids, Michigan. However, she also had been drawn to a life of missions. Before I met her, Helen had indicated to the Board of World Missions of our denomination her interest in serving as a

Chapter One: The Calling

Christian teacher in Taiwan. Now, here we were driving westward, headed towards our mission.

THE LAND I WILL SHOW YOU

After a long day, we stopped for the night in North Platte, Nebraska. The next day was hot. As we moved into western Nebraska and then Wyoming, the temperature reached 105 degrees. I had never experienced anything like this. The landscape began changing into wide-open country with gentle rolling hills covered with tall, dead grass. We passed through the cities of Cheyenne and Laramie in Wyoming. This was cowboy country. Now and then there would be large herds of beef cattle, and you could sometimes make out a homestead in the far distance. Helen and I discussed how those ranchers lived a lonely life, and we began to wonder about the lives of the people we were about to minister to, the Navajo Indians. Passing through those desolate areas, I was thankful to live in a time of grocery stores and butcher shops, but I wondered if the Navajo people were familiar with our comforts and luxuries of life.

I literally knew nothing about Navajos, except for what Helen had told me. What little she knew came from reading articles in *The Banner*, our church's news magazine, and from a trip she had previously taken to the Navajo and Zuni mission field in New Mexico. She told me the Navajos were mostly ranchers, raising mostly sheep, and also doing a little farming. I couldn't help but wonder how I, someone who had grown up on a small farm in the Netherlands, was supposed to minister to a bunch of "cowboy Indians."

As a child, I had observed Home Missions at work in Canada and was impressed with their dedicated service of reaching out to immigrant families and gathering people into churches. Six months had passed since the two of us had made our initial visit to the Home Mission office to indicate our desire to work with them. We were well received and told there might soon be an opening for us to serve as church planters in the Peace River Valley of Alberta, Canada at a place called Blueberry Mountain. This all sounded good to us. To serve in a rural community in my adopted

Chapter One: The Calling

country Canada among farm people like ourselves was immediately appealing, as was the job of gathering people into a church. Then another candidate was offered the job—the Lord had shut that door on us.

It was then that we were told of another opening among the Navajo Indians. Our initial reaction to mission work with the Navajo was not very enthusiastic. The work consisted of giving Bible instruction and counseling to a large group of Navajo students at Intermountain Indian School in Brigham City, Utah. With my Bible training and major in sociology, the Mission Board felt this work might be just right for me. It took time to think this through and pray about it, and as time went by, our enthusiasm began to grow. We were both asked to undergo a psychiatric test and then meet for an interview at the Board's annual meeting. We were chosen for the work in Brigham City. I was deeply touched by this meeting as the delegates offered a prayer of thanksgiving to God for us and wished us the blessings of the Lord. A few days later I received a telephone call from Rev. Casey Kuipers, pastor at Brigham City. He and his wife then met with us while on vacation in Grand Rapids. The meeting was very helpful and enlightening. The two gave us much encouragement, especially when they assured us they believed we were the right candidates for the job.

Now, as we spent our third night on the road in Rawlins, Wyoming, we were just one day away. Sore and stiff from all the sitting in the car, we nonetheless left the next morning with a decided feeling of anticipation. Just west of the town of Rock Springs, our highway divided into U.S. Highways 30 South and 30 North. While both directions ultimately could take us to our destination, the Southern route went towards Salt Lake City and Ogden. Wishing to avoid city traffic, we went north. Soon we were passing through sagebrush country. It had been raining lightly in the area, and the smell of the sage was quite strong, but refreshing. This would become one of the most recognizable smells of home for many years to come in the Southwest.

Mile after mile, we wove our way across the hills and through the valleys. As we saw Utah's Bear Lake from miles away in the mountains, we thought it looked like a beautiful picture we had seen

Chapter One: The Calling

somewhere of the Sea of Galilee nestled between the mountains of Northern Israel. We passed through Logan Canyon, a gorgeous land of mountains, forest, and sparkling streams of clear water. Driving was slow and tense for people like us who were not used to mountain driving. And then we saw in the distance a large, flat basin. Unmistakably, it was the valley of the Great Salt Lake. This was the valley where the Mormons had settled over a century before of which their leader, Brigham Young, said, "This is the place."

Hopefully, this would be the place where people would make room for us newcomers in our new home and new mission.

Brigham City Intermountain School

CHAPTER 2

Utah

BRIGHAM CITY

We found the house that would be ours to live in. As we had already been told, my predecessor and his family had not completed moving out of it yet. They were busy packing and getting ready for a move to Nigeria. In the meantime, temporary arrangements had been made for us to stay in a small kitchenette unit at a local motel. This would be our home for the first week, allowing time for the house to be vacated as well as for our furniture to arrive. It was a workable arrangement for us, even though the room was very small and hot, without air conditioning.

We were surprised to hear that a cousin of mine had called the motel office and said that he was on his way to visit us. He had come hitchhiking across the U.S. from Ontario and was on his way to nearby Salt Lake City, where he wanted to investigate the Mormon religion. Having heard that we had moved to Brigham City, he decided to look us up. He spent a day with us and together we did some of the initial sightseeing of the area. He and I even managed to climb up the mountain ridge on the east side of town.

There was little activity at the church that week. Rev. Kuipers was gone camping with a youth group from the church. Things were also very quiet at the Intermountain Indian School as well since the students were all at home on the reservation for the summer months. My work would really begin in August after the students returned to school. In the meantime, these weeks before school were to serve to orient me to my work and to read about the Navajo and cross-cultural problems they had to face. They were in the minority here. The people of Utah would not look like them or share their exact value systems. Many would not know the language well at all. The food, the sights, and the sounds would all be different from that of home.

Chapter Two: Utah

I became somewhat restless in our motel room that first week. There must have been too much adrenaline running through me to be able to relax. I was eager to get working. Rev. Kuipers had asked me to meet with the youth camping in Logan Canyon to lead them in their devotion time at the evening campfire. They were some of the children of the community and Navajo Intermountain School employees. I spoke on David and Goliath. The following day, I joined them on a long hike in the mountains. It was a fun experience, as camping was something new to me. I even remember that one of the boys was unable to find his shoes that morning. He seemed unconcerned about the problem and joined us hiking on socks. Apparently he had not grown up to be as tenderfooted as many of the rest of us might have been. It didn't take too long before those socks were filthy and full of holes. That evening, the group and I enjoyed a great meal of mutton chops in the open mountain air.

Back at the motel the following day, I decided to do some evangelism by visiting some homes in the community. It would give me an opportunity to invite children to an upcoming Vacation Bible School at the church. The population of Brigham City was about 70% Mormon. These were people who had no clear knowledge of the true Christian message of salvation through Jesus Christ.

Little did I know how quickly my devotional on David and Goliath was to become so appropriate. An older lady invited me into her home. She seemed to be truly interested in what I shared with her. She urged me strongly to return that evening so that we could continue our conversation. When I returned, I was surprised to see two men in white shirts and ties sitting in the living room. The lady had invited some Mormon church leaders to confront me. The one introduced himself as an elder, even though he seemed to be younger than even I was. The other said that he was a bishop in the church. They were eager for me to explain why I had come to visit at the house of the lady. I told them of my desire to share the gospel of Jesus with his people.

The two men assured me that the Mormon people already had Jesus *and* that their understanding of the gospel was superior to mine. Not wanting to get into a big argument that would

Chapter Two: Utah

end nowhere, I mentioned that a Christian is at least assured of his salvation. This seemed to be a topic that was somewhat uncomfortable for them. They mentioned, in turn, that their main assurance was that Joseph Smith was a true prophet of God and that their church was the true church. I replied with John 3:16, saying that my confidence was in Jesus and in the sacrifice he had made to pay for my sin. As a result of receiving Him as my Lord and Savior, I would never perish but have eternal life. After this, I got up, said goodbye, and left the house. This visit served to remind me that there was an enemy who would oppose any attempt to reach people for Jesus. It also gave me an interest in learning more about the Mormon faith so that I would understand them better. They were a people whose God was their church, but not the Lord Jesus.

Two days later there was a happier visit for me. A mother and her children invited me in and asked questions about our Bible School and our church. To my amazement, they all attended our worship service the next Sunday and the children registered for our Bible school a week later. Eventually, this family committed themselves to Jesus and became members of our church.

After a week in the motel, it was finally time to settle into our house. Our furniture had by now arrived and been stored in the garage. Now everything had to be put in place. We were living in a new residential area. Many of our neighbors had moved in from other parts of the country and were employed at a rocket factory just north of town. There they manufactured rocket engines, and at certain times we could hear the roar of those engines when they were tested.

The house was a tri-level and new. The downstairs was occupied by Lena Benally, my terrific co-worker. As a Navajo, she was very helpful with ministry to Navajo students. She had good knowledge of the Navajo culture and spoke the language, which was a great advantage. Our little family still had plenty of room on the second and third level of the house and it seemed as if we would be living lavishly.

Since there was even room for an office, I took a trip to the local lumberyard to get a few boards to make some shelves for it. To my surprise, the cashier asked me if I was a Mormon. I replied,

Chapter Two: Utah

"No." She explained that this was too bad because they give a 10% discount to only their Mormon customers. Although I did not appreciate the obvious discrimination, I felt honored to pay the full amount.

As part of our orientation, we were encouraged to spend a week in Phoenix, Arizona to attend a conference that dealt with Native American culture, including the Navajo. After the meeting in Phoenix, there would be a meeting of the Indian General Conference at Rehoboth, New Mexico, just south of the Navajo Reservation. This was a gathering of all the mission personnel of our churches and mission stations on the reservation. At this meeting, all matters pertaining to the mission work of the Christian Reformed Church to the Navajo were being discussed. The work in Brigham City was considered as part of that, even though it was off-reservation work.

We traveled to Phoenix with the Bakkers, who headed the Christian Indian Center in Salt Lake City. Though we would have preferred to leave in the morning, Mr. Bakker had to first lead a funeral service. This postponed our trip to the heat of the afternoon. The funeral also brought an additional inconvenience. A family who attended was unable to get back home on the reservation and was looking for a ride. In the end, all nine people—our family, theirs, and the Bakkers—crowded into a station wagon, creating quite a tight fit after all of our luggage was added. Though it was nice to be able to help the family get back home, it was also a relief to now have more space in the vehicle.

The week spent in Phoenix was good, but the 115 degree heat was almost unbearable. Helen and I decided that it would never be our choice to live in that city in the summer months. After the conference was over, there was a little extra time to do some sightseeing. We traveled through Oak Creek Canyon near Flagstaff and went to see the Grand Canyon. The scenery was gorgeous! It all pointed to a creator with power, wisdom and beauty. From there, the Bakkers went home, but Helen, Jack, and I traveled by bus to Rehoboth. From there we would eventually ride home with the other members of the Brigham City staff.

The meeting of the Indian General Conference was an eye-opener for me. It was obvious, even to a newcomer like myself, that something was not right. The meeting was led by white missionaries with surprisingly little participation from the Navajo. Most of the native men and women were quietly seated and they observed from the back of the audience. The whites were doing most of the talking and voting on issues that dealt with the mission field. The discussions were held in English for the most part and the Roberts Rules of Order were strictly observed. There also seemed to be an attempt to make a distinction between "ordained clergy", "unordained lay workers", those who "preached" the word of God, and those who only "exhorted" it. All of this discrimination felt wrong. There was a sense of injustice in that room that bothered me. Having grown up in an immigrant family, I knew what it was like to be discriminated against. There seemed to be some of that same discrimination at the meeting, though unintentionally so. Even though I had little to contribute to the deliberations, I was glad of the learning experience it provided.

As I was settling in for the work ahead, I began to get to know Rev. Kuipers. He would be my mentor for the first 6 months of my ministry. I grew to have a great respect for the man, the kind of respect that seemed to follow him everywhere he went.

Casey Kuipers had originally been the principal at Zuni Christian School some 40 miles south of Gallup, NM on the Zuni Reservation. After his first wife passed away and he had remarried, he became an ordained minister in the Christian Reformed denomination, working at the mission in Zuni for a number of years. While ordination was required by the denomination for the work he was doing, he never felt much personal importance in the formality of being ordained. He believed that if you were called to serve in a certain way, then you should do it. Nor did he confine his ministry solely to the CRC, but reached out to work with Christians from all denominations. He also did some work among the Navajo in the more southern outlying areas of the Navajo Reservation. From there, his ministry moved to Utah where he ministered in Salt Lake City and then Brigham City.

Kuipers was important to my development as a pastor as I watched him work and learned from him. First and foremost, he

Chapter Two: Utah

was an encouragement to me, a man cut from the same mold as Barnabas. As I toiled through that first year, he was never critical, always having something encouraging to say to lift me up and give me the confidence that I would be able to complete the task the Lord had given me. He was a great man of prayer. He was also very patriotic, as I remember that he would always raise the U.S. flag at the start and end of every day at the church, saluting it both times.

Gary and Helen with baby Jack.

DIGGING IN

It was at the end of August when the Navajo students returned to the Intermountain Indian School. A long row of yellow school buses unloaded their precious occupants after the long ride from the reservation where the children had spent their summer vacation at home. They all looked tired, and some of them bewildered. While some were older and in their teens, there were also many little ones of five or six years of age. What a traumatic experience it must have been for those little ones! They had been taken away from the security of home and family to live at a government boarding school for nine months at a time. They were strangers in a strange land.

Chapter Two: Utah

My heart was touched as I joined to greet them. I felt like hugging those beautiful little children. These were the ones I was asked to counsel and with whom the gospel of Jesus was to be shared. I began to ask myself some questions that I had begun to wonder about: Was this the best way to educate Native American children? Was it not important for them to experience home and family? Was that not an important part of a child's education? And why were these children taken so far away from home?

There were several government boarding schools throughout the country, but Intermountain School was the largest of them all. Many people, as well as the U.S. government, believed that in order to give an effective education to these children, they had to be removed from their own culture. It was thought that such children would learn better how to compete successfully later in life and to master the English language. Even some of the Christian churches and mission schools on the reservation supported such ideas and were being, in my opinion, culturally insensitive. We had even heard that at some mission schools, the children were forbidden to speak the Navajo language and punished if caught doing so.

The Mormon Church, in particular, was working hard at robbing native children of their language and culture. They also worked at the school and had about 300 students attending the Mormon Center. They even set up a placement program where native children would be taken away from their home and live with a Mormon family in Utah. The native aspect in these children was seen as a negative thing that would hinder their development. Some leaders of the Mormon Church, or the "LDS"—Latter Day Saints—as church members are often referred to, even taught that the longer a native had been a member of the Mormon Church, the whiter his children's skin would become until they reached heaven, where their skin would be pure white. The dark skin was a sign of a curse that needed to be removed as much as possible—if not on the outside, then surely on the inside.

Once school was in full swing, all students were released for religious instruction classes on a certain day of the week. Students went to the church of their parent's choice. The Christian Reformed Church had a long history of bringing the gospel to the Navajo

Chapter Two: Utah

people and over the years had established several churches and mission posts. The denomination had worked mainly on the part of the reservation that is in New Mexico, where it had become the dominant church and was well known by the people. For this reason, about 400 students at the school were registered by their parents as belonging to the Christian Reformed Church, even though many of them had never seen the inside of a church before. As an indication of how little he knew of the church, one of the students mistakenly wrote that he belonged to the "Christmas Form" church. We were grateful to the Lord for giving us the opportunity to give instruction to so many in the Christian faith and even to be permitted to counsel them when needed.

After school hours, two afternoons per week, as well as some evenings, we held Bible classes at the church. The older students came one day and the younger ones the next. It was a big job to find proper teaching materials as several children spoke little English and could hardly read it. It was part of my job to obtain the proper materials and also to arrange for teachers willing to teach. Members of the Brigham City and Ogden churches graciously volunteered for this work, besides our own church staff. With the encouragement of the school, most of the students attended Bible classes faithfully each week.

The older students were often served a cup of hot coffee before class. This was an incentive for them to come. Back home they were used to drinking a lot of coffee and had done so ever since they were small, but, at school, no coffee was served and the students missed it. Lena, my co-worker, was an expert at making frybread, and there were times when the students were also served some at the church. The hot grease left a heavy smell in the church building, but the children loved it.

On Sunday mornings, the older students were given special permission to attend worship services. In the evenings, they could join our "church choir" which I directed (even though I knew very little about music) if they so desired and had a record of good behavior. We had a group of about 35 teenagers in our group. Singing was popular with them and a new venture for some. Carrying a tune was often a skill that had to be learned. In their

Chapter Two: Utah

native setting, only Christian people learned to sing. The only sort of singing besides that would have been the chanting of the medicine men. The students loved to learn to sing songs in the Navajo language. They also enjoyed wearing the red choir robes that had been sent by a church out east. Most of these used robes were much too large for our students. With the kind help of some of the church ladies, the robes were made to fit better. Our "choir" even managed to give a special presentation one Sunday evening in one of the Salt Lake City churches. I'll never forget how well they sang that night, full of joyous enthusiasm. I was so proud of them. Years later, I met some of these students again. They told us that the singing in the choir had affected them deeply as the joy they got from it drew them further into the Christian life.

It took a little time to get used to teaching the Bible classes. At first, many of the students seemed to look very much alike. It took time to get a handle on such strange names as Tsinniginnie and Todacheene. We also had to learn that some students had a large number of "brothers" and "sisters" at the school. In their culture, the children of their mother's sisters were regarded as their siblings. The same was true for the children of their father's brothers. It was not uncommon for a student to tell us that he did not know for sure the exact number of brothers and sisters he had.

We had some language difficulties as well. The use of double negatives had to be avoided since they confused the students. At the time of the roll call in one of my classes, a student appeared to be absent. In order to be sure, I said to the class, "Sam isn't here, is he?" The students responded "yes", meaning, "Yes, he isn't here." I naturally replied, "Where is he then?" With a confused look on their faces, they said, "He isn't here." Several times in life I have thanked the Lord that English is my second language like it was for many of the Navajo. It helped me to identify with the difficulties people of a different language have in understanding some English slang, idioms, out-of-date words, and other irregularities. After all—it *is* strange that we speak of horses and cows, but not sheeps. Some old wives' tales, such as one which says that good weather is coming if you sneeze, is meaningless to the Navajo in that Navajo tradition instead says that a sneeze means that someone is talking

Chapter Two: Utah

about you. I had heard of a missionary who once preached on Jesus and the children in Mark 10:13-16, using the old King James Version of the Bible. He mentioned how Jesus had said, "Suffer the little children to come to me..." and neglected to explain the now archaic meaning of the word "suffer" to his Navajo congregation. The interpreter, misunderstanding the meaning, gave a literal interpretation into the Navajo language, telling them that little children had to do a lot of suffering if they wanted to come to Jesus.

The Lord did bless our feeble efforts as we presented the gospel of Jesus. Some of the seeds of faith that we planted began to grow with the blessing of the Lord. On a few occasions, a group of ten or more confessed publicly that they had received Jesus as their Lord and Savior. They were baptized and joined the membership of the church, always a joyous occasion.

Helen and I started Bible lessons at our home with a young couple who were former students at the school. From them we learned important things about the Navajo religion and culture. This was beneficial for us later when we moved to the reservation to work there. The couple told us of the powers of a medicine man. We came to understand that such power was not superstition, but real power—and evil power. They told us of experiences they had had with the wolf man and with frightening skinwalkers who came around at night to hurt people. This couple had seen their tracks in the sand—no mere ghosts or dreams. They were certain that their pack of watchdogs had scared them off, however. Another time, while driving on one of the highways, they had seen a wolf man running next to their car, matching them at a speed of 60 mph.

We did not know how to deal with all of this information at that time. One thing we knew for sure, though, was that this couple sharing this with us was not manufacturing lies. We would later hear many similar stories from believers and nonbelievers alike in the coming years, and we would learn even more of things pertaining to the demonic world—and how to deal with them.

The second summer in Brigham City, Helen, Jack, and I spent a two-week vacation in Yellowstone National Park. Part of our time there was spent in preparing new Bible lessons for the students. Helen's training as a teacher came in handy in this part of the

Chapter Two: Utah

ministry. We did our utmost to make the lessons more sensitive to the needs of our students and managed to make some good lessons. We had a good time there, as Yellowstone was a great change of scenery for us.

It even provided at least one very memorable experience. The park was notorious, especially then, for all the wild bears that were roaming around freely. While at an outdoor church service there, three large grizzlies came strutting up the center aisle towards the stage. They then proceeded to walk politely out again. Everyone there wisely kept their distance from the unexpected visitors. The worship service had quite an interruption, to say the least.

Back at the school, as I gained more confidence, I also began to enjoy times when I was asked to counsel with students. Some of the students were suffering from homesickness. They missed their parents and family on the reservation. These students needed a lot of love and attention. The little ones in particular needed a lot of assurance. It was wonderful to be able to remind them that Jesus would take care of them. We would pray together and I sometimes had to dry a lot of tears. I believe that it was there that the Lord gave me a deep love for the Navajo that has never left me. I learned to hurt with them.

During that second year, things at church got pretty busy for a while as Rev. Kuipers was retiring from the ministry. He would be missed, but he had also done much to prepare me for the work that lay ahead. Everywhere he had been, Kuipers had built a terrific reputation and was well-liked. After he left, a former neighbor of his asked me where the pastor had gone. When I told him that the pastor had retired, he said to me, "He sure was a good man—too good not to be a Mormon."

Even after Kuipers left, he continued to be a blessing to me, occasionally coming to visit with me to see how we were doing and to encourage me. I would be honored by him many years later when he personally asked me to be one of two pastors who would conduct his funeral service.

It was six months before Kuipers was replaced. In the meantime, I was asked to do more preaching at our church and, occasionally, at Ogden and Salt Lake City. Public speaking had always come easy to me. It was one of the college courses that I was able to get an A in without too much difficulty. But to preach the Word of God was more than to give a speech, and I had no formal training in that. Regardless, necessity required me to fill the role. On Saturday mornings, I would go to church when it was safely empty to practice my sermon from the pulpit. I remember, however, being embarrassed one Saturday as a visiting family from Iowa walked into the sanctuary while I practiced in front of the empty chairs. They had heard loud preaching and were curious to see what could be going on. I was somewhat embarrassed, even though I did not need to be. Even more difficult was the 30-minute program that our church put on the local radio station on Sunday mornings. I was expected to present a fifteen minute meditation. Speaking into a microphone felt uncomfortable to me. When Rev. Mulder came to serve as our new pastor, I was grateful that he took over all of these duties from me.

Al Mulder was a pastor in Luctor, Kansas when he was called to serve in Brigham City. He was particularly gifted in organization and well suited for working with emerging churches. After serving in Brigham City for 4 years, he would serve as pastor at Gallup Christian Reformed Church, very near the reservation, for the next 16 years, and thereafter serving as staff in the CRC Home Missions Office. He would be instrumental in my call to serve as missionary on the reservation.

Mulder's arrival was a relief to me. Now I was free to help out a little with a group of former students in Ogden who were meeting together each week. I was able to lead a Bible study for them on Wednesdays and meet with them for some recreation on Saturday evenings. I remember that it was from these people that I would learn to eat and enjoy watermelon for the first time, a food that I had yet to become accustomed to.

HEART TROUBLE

Helen has always been an integral part of my ministry and we worked together as much as possible. She was teaching Bible classes weekly at Intermountain School, again using her training in education to her advantage. She also had a Bible class at the church for children of the community. In our living room, she held a "Good News Club" every week for children in our new housing area. This club consisted of three different classes per week for three different age groups. This kept her quite busy, beyond her duties as a mother and homemaker.

However, throughout her second pregnancy during that first year in Brigham City, she was suffering from extreme tiredness. Eventually this became so bad that whenever she went up the six steps in our house between the second and third levels, she needed to pause halfway up to catch her breath. We went to the doctor who discovered that she was suffering from rheumatic heart disease. Her heart's mitral valve had grown almost completely shut. This explained why, as a child, she always had difficulty running any distance or riding her bicycle up a hill. Those problems had never been diagnosed at that time as a matter of any concern.

In early October, A few weeks after our second son, David, was born, Helen went into heart failure and was rushed to the hospital. With such a disruption to our work and having to care for an infant and a seventeen-month-old, we were grateful that my youngest sister, Rita, came from Canada to help us during this time. She was only seventeen years old, but very efficient in the home and wonderful with our two small children.

Helen regained her strength after two weeks in the hospital and was able to return home. About a month later, my sister returned home since Helen was able to manage things again without help. Quite soon after this, however, Helen began showing signs of going back into heart failure. It became clear that medication was unable to take care of the problem as we had hoped. Open heart surgery was now necessary.

At that time, this surgery was rather new and risky. The doctors told us that the success rate for such procedures was about 50%. Fortunately, a hospital in Salt Lake City was one of the major heart centers in the nation, with the best equipment available and some of the finest doctors trained in the latest techniques. We told the doctor that we were not insured for such an expensive surgery and could not afford it, but he replied that we had no choice. Somehow the surgery would be made affordable for us.

Chapter Two: Utah

Rita, who had just settled in back home in Canada, promptly repacked her suitcase and came out for a second time. For a few days, in the meantime, our children were lovingly cared for by members of our church. At night, the baby stayed with me at home. I would do a lot of traveling between Brigham City and Salt Lake City in those days, a distance of sixty miles. It would take a couple of weeks for Helen to regain her strength before surgery could take place. In all that time and distance, I learned to do a lot of praying.

On one of my trips to the hospital, I felt a deep sense of loneliness and self-despair, even though I knew that I should have been feeling a greater concern over Helen than myself. While driving that evening, the tears began to stream down my face. I pleaded there to the Lord to spare the life of my wife, the mother of my two small children. How could I ever manage without her? Then I noticed that the western sky was gloriously painted in a beautiful sunset. It was a reminder to me that the Lord was there with me and that He was in complete control of all things, including our problems. This gave me a wonderful assurance that supported me in days to come.

With Christmas fast approaching, the doctors told Helen that she could spend Christmas Day at home with the family if she so desired. They would perform surgery immediately after her return to the hospital. Although the offer to go home was tempting, she refused, fearing more heart failure. They decided then to do the surgery two days before Christmas.

Our farewell came the evening before the next morning's surgery. Helen asked me to join her in prayer to ask God to give her the blessing of seeing her two children grow up. We prayed together, and as I was about to leave, she said, "Things will be all right. Remember that, even if we do not see each other again on earth, we'll be together forever in glory." Those words kept ringing in my ears that night. I was proud of my wife who showed greater courage than I myself could muster.

It was a six-hour-surgery. For the first five hours, I sat alone in the waiting room without getting any report on the surgery. They were long hours. It was only reassuring to me that Helen was not sharing in my anxiety. I was also thankful for three volunteers from the Salt Lake City churches who were somewhere in the hospital to serve as on-the-spot blood donors. In the last hour, I finally heard that the surgery had been successful.

Later, I would find out that the surgery revealed a bigger problem than anticipated. One chamber of the heart was filled with blood clots. The doctor explained later that it was providential that they hadn't waited with the surgery until after Christmas and that it was very good that Helen had not gone back home. A blood clot could easily have escaped from the heart and lodged in her brain resulting in a stroke, and possibly death. It was clear evidence to me that the Lord was watching over us. The doctor commented, "I do not want the credit for the apparent success of this surgery. This was the work of hands that are greater than mine."

Much of the dreaded cost of the surgery was canceled, having been absorbed by the doctors and the hospital. This is a clear reminder that, despite the differences in beliefs, the Mormon people—many of whom worked there—can be very good people. They were very good to us at that time, something for which we have always been grateful. Another one thousand dollars was also generously contributed by the Board of Home Missions to help cover the costs. The remaining portion of the cost we were able to pay off over the next five years. The Lord does provide for those who trust in Him. He is a Mighty Rock for those who lean on Him. Often we have told people how the experience of having to go through that crisis was actually good for us. It brought us closer to the Lord and served to prepare us for more ministry in the years ahead. We were better able to help and empathize with others in their times of difficulty.

Helen's recovery was amazing. Three days after surgery, she was able to walk a little, and a week later she was able to go home to recuperate further. Soon she began to feel stronger than she had in a long time. Helen has now lived to see all of her children grow up, marry, and have children. The surgery kept Helen healthy for the next twenty-five years.

SALT LAKE CITY

A large number of Intermountain School students, when

Chapter Two: Utah

they graduated, chose to move to Salt Lake City where they could more easily find employment. Back home on the reservation, it was almost impossible for young people to find a job, and the rate of unemployment was around 60%. Most of these young people started their own families in Salt Lake City, got their first jobs there, and ultimately settled throughout the city. A larger number of them lived in the poorer areas of town where the rent for housing was more affordable. Our mission board hired a missionary to locate these young families and try to work them into a Christian group for Navajo people. This group eventually became known as the Christian Indian Center.

The Christian Indian Center held its meetings in the basement of the Christian School. There they held social events, potluck dinners, midweek Bible classes, and the Sunday worship services. There they could socialize with each other and, more importantly, they could worship and grow in the faith together. The Center had its attraction for many, as sometimes the Navajos found it pretty difficult to cope with learning to live in the land of the White man.

When the missionary position at the Center became vacant, the Mission Board offered me that position. It seemed too soon, however, for us to leave Brigham City. We had not even been there three years. I notified the Board that we preferred to stay on at Brigham City for a while. The Mission Board, though, was insistent and asked me to divide my time between working at the Christian Indian Center and Brigham City. For the next six months, I split my workload, spending my Fridays through Sundays in Salt Lake City and the rest in Brigham City.

The longer I worked in Salt Lake City, the more I grew to enjoy the work there. I enjoyed making visits with families and leading them in a time of worship. Once again the Mission Board asked me to consider the vacancy, and this time we accepted. On Helen's birthday in February of 1966, we moved into a house in the Sugarhouse neighborhood of Salt Lake City, the very heart of Mormon Country—or, as they say, "in the shadow of the Tabernacle."

There were two CRC churches in Salt Lake City, both with which the Christian Indian Center was affiliated. Many of the non-native members of these churches were of Dutch descent and recent immigrants to the U.S. The earliest of these immigrants had been encouraged by LDS missionaries in Europe to immigrate to Utah with the promise of assistance from the Mormon church. Believing that the Mormons were a fundamentally sound Christian church, they became very disappointed once they came to Utah. Eventually, many pulled out of the LDS and joined the strongly Dutch-oriented Christian Reformed denomination.

As time went by, other families joined them, including Navajos who had been reached with the gospel by the denomination elsewhere. The big obsession in our denomination and mission board became the need for different cultural groups to become integrated. Our Navajo group was required to be integrated into the two CRC's there. This idea seemed right to me, although I knew it was a big order to fill. There were plenty of reasons to believe this would be hard to accomplish. The cultural differences were very evident.

The Navajo people seemed to have fewer problems with the integration than did the Whites. The Navajo were used to integration—they did it every day in their workplaces. It was harder for the other side to reach out to the Navajo. The Whites seemed more set in their traditional ways of worship, practices still mostly foreign to the Navajo. Still, initial steps at integration into the local churches were taken. The groups began to hold worship services together on Sundays. All the children and some of the adults had Sunday school classes together. We did hold separate Bible study groups in the afternoon, however, and the Center continued to hold its regular Friday night meetings. From time to time, some of the Whites at the churches would join our group for a potluck dinner in a positive attempt to make connections and friends. All in all, things worked as well as could be expected, but never really as well as hoped. A few years later, the attempt at integration was discontinued and the Navajo group met separately as they had before, and as they still do today.

When not overseeing activities at the Center, I spent much of my time spreading the Gospel to Navajos living in Bingham Canyon, about 25 miles west of Salt Lake City. Some Navajo people

Chapter Two: Utah

had found employment at the copper mine there. These people had come directly from the reservation in search of jobs. The mining company provided housing for them, but the houses were little more than wooden shacks. Each Thursday, I would travel to visit these families. Since some of these people spoke very limited English, if any, I took someone with me who served as my interpreter. At those visits we shared Bible messages. Some ladies met together in a home for a Bible study. It was an interesting work. It would help connect me closer to the more traditional Navajo people with whom I would be working in the years ahead. I particularly noticed their interest in spiritual things and an openness to learning what the Bible had to tell them.

The people I worked with in Salt Lake City were faced with a variety of problems, many related to the general difficulties of bridging the cultural divide. Some met discrimination at their jobs. Others could not afford to make their monthly payments. Still others had built up too much credit card debt. Some had little experience in saving money and therefore could not make the paycheck last from one payday to the next. Yet others lived in a rented facility where the rent was outrageously high while the building was hardly kept up by the owners. Finally, there was the problem of alcohol abuse, which resulted in family discord and, occasionally, jail time. This last problem in particular plagued the Navajo in general, and had devastating effects on the reservation. It was a problem I would come to recognize well in our time of serving the Navajo people.

During the summer, we scheduled a one-week Vacation Bible School for children in the Bingham Canyon area. In Bingham Canyon, there were a few old picnic tables that we could use, but there were no water or bathroom facilities. It was, though, a quiet area and free from traffic. Some of the members of First Christian Reformed Church of Salt Lake City volunteered to help and transport the children. All the workbooks, craft materials, and snacks had to be brought out there each day. One summer, we had Helen's former college roommate and her cousin come and help us. It was hard work, as always, but also fun, and we believe that VBS served to get the gospel of Jesus to children and their families.

Chapter Two: Utah

Not all the families were interested in our Bible School. Most of those affiliated with the Mormon Church were under pressure from their church not to associate with us. Some simply lacked interest in any sort of Christian activity. People would sometimes do interesting things to avoid it. I knocked on the door of one house, recruiting children for Bible School, when I heard some whispering inside. A young boy eventually opened the door and announced, "My mother says she isn't home." More often, people would simply tell me they couldn't attend because they were Mormon, whether it was true or not.

From time to time, I was called on by others to help out Native Americans in the community who were in need of assistance. Once, a local pastor called to inform me that he had met a Native American man who appeared to be in need of just such help. He hoped that I would visit the man and gave me an address.

I found the man in a room on the fourth floor of an old hotel. He introduced himself as "Johnny" and said that he was a member of the Blackfoot Tribe in Idaho. He seemed to be genuinely happy to see me and said that he was interested in learning about the Christian life. He also showed me a card for his employer, a local lumberyard. Unfortunately, he had to be away from his wife, who was ill, and children to earn a living to support them. He was low on food and needed help. He asked me to meet with him one evening per week to give him a Bible lesson. I agreed to help him the best I could. We prayed together and I left him a check for twenty-five dollars.

A few days later, when we had agreed to meet together, he was not in his room. I became a bit suspicious. Could I have been perhaps fooled by a crook? I thought of the story of Joshua and the Gibeonites when Joshua had neglected to ask God for His guidance when he was being deceived. I had neglected to ask for God's guidance as well. I went home and, the following morning, I called the lumberyard where Johnny was employed. To my surprise, no one there had ever seen or heard of him. My suspicion grew even larger, so I called the Roman Catholic Social Services where they dealt with many homeless people. They did know a "Johnny" and told me not to trust him as he had been going to various churches for free handouts using untrue stories to gain sympathy. It was then clear that I had been fooled.

Still, I went back to his hotel room that evening. Again, Johnny was not there to answer the door, but as I descended the long flight of stairs, the front door suddenly swung open. There came my man, running up the stairs towards me. Barely noticing me, he said, "Come back next week."

No sooner was he out of sight, when two police officers came storming in. Out of breath, they asked me, "Where is that man?"

"He's in room 403," I answered.

Johnny, it turned out, was wanted for holding up some people at knife point. The officers found a knife on him and handcuffed him as I watched. As they took him down to the police cruiser, I walked up to Johnny and told him, "What a man sows, that shall he also reap." He said nothing, but his face showed the anger he held inside. From there he was taken away. I thanked God for the lessons He had taught me through this episode and for sparing my life from harm that could have been done to me by an apparently violent criminal. From my heart came a prayer: "Lord, change that man and also bring him to Your wonderful salvation."

During the summer months, some of the students at Intermountain School had found employment in Salt Lake City. They preferred to work and earn some money instead of spending the summer on the reservation with nothing to do. A number of these students were referred to us so that we could make contact with them and transport them to the Christian Indian Center on Sundays for worship. Occasionally, a student had to be dismissed from his job. Sometimes he would stay at our house until other arrangements could be made for him. It was gratifying to see that most of these students did well at their summer jobs.

With the time we were spending with the Navajo, and they with us, it became clear that many of the people we were ministering to lacked wholesome recreation. In the city there was no horseback riding or rodeo activity as there was to occupy their time on the reservation. We introduced group activities which they were generally unacquainted with as of yet, such as bowling, miniature golf, and even fishing.

Sometimes we would be joined on these outings by others in the community who, although not Native American, were still culturally outsiders in the city, such as the time an Indonesian couple joined us on our first bowling outing. They, being unfamiliar with the sport as well, had some learning to do. It was the Indonesian man, then, who first experienced the difficulty one might have in choosing a ball which your fingers will not get stuck in as you release it towards the pins. On his turn, he lost his balance as he heaved the ball forward, rolling himself right onto the bowling lane. You could see the other bowlers from other parties in the establishment looking us over, wondering what kind of fools we must have been. Nonetheless, we had a great time and lots of laughter to go with it. Bowling became a favorite activity of our group.

Some men joined me fishing one day as well. We rented a rowboat and fished on Strawberry Lake. Although it was a new experience for them, we all enjoyed ourselves, despite a limited catch of rainbow trout. Some of them had never tasted fish before, an unpopular and uncommon food on the reservation. I, on the other hand, loved to fish and was glad to share the experience, as well as any others with them. My connections with the Navajo people were growing steadily stronger all the while.

"COME OVER AND HELP US"

Helen, in the meantime, continued to be blessed with a wonderful recovery. She was doing so well that the doctors told us that there was no valid reason why we could not entertain the thought of having more children. It was on April 30, 1968, that our third son, Jim, joined our family. Helen experienced no complications during her pregnancy or at the time of the birth. God had certainly been good to us.

I had a lingering issue with which to deal. Throughout college, I followed a pre-seminary course of study with the intention of eventually attending seminary. Whereas Public Speaking had been a breeze to pass, my problem was that I could not manage to pass the required course in Greek. Three times I tried, and three times I failed. Eventually, it was decided that I should major in Sociology, supplemented by adequate Bible training. It was not enough to get

Chapter Two: Utah

me an official license to preach, but hopefully the Lord would still put me to work in ministry. I trusted that the Lord still had a place of ministry for me, and I had found it so far in Utah.

The Utah churches, though, were still often in need of someone who could serve as a guest pastor in times of need. They encouraged me to take some more training in Bible doctrine and other church matters. I accepted the challenge, resulting in my oral examination at a meeting of Classis Rocky Mountain, of which the Utah churches were a part. The license was granted and opportunity to be of service was broadened.

Soon after this, rumors began to go around that we were now under consideration for a new position—on the Navajo Reservation itself. Although the idea of working there did have some appeal, we were content in Salt Lake City, for the Lord was blessing our mission there. We had seen some people we worked with come to faith in Jesus. There were indications of spiritual growth among the members of our group. Besides that, we had developed a good rapport with the people and made some very dear friends among them. For us, there was no reason to look for greener pastures.

In November of 1968, we received official notice from our mission board that they were considering us for work on the reservation in Toadlena, New Mexico. The steering committee of the Toadlena Church had voted between two possible candidates that had been proposed to them by the mission board. I was the chosen one of the two. Later, I learned that they chose me because the other man was a smoker. Little did they know that I was a light smoker myself earlier in my lifetime, but had stopped the habit knowing that it was detrimental in my work as a missionary, as well as a threat to my health.

The mission board suggested that I spend a weekend in Toadlena to become more familiar with the mission there. I would have an opportunity to meet the Toadlena congregation and lead them in a worship service. This seemed wise and would have a mutual benefit for us and for the Toadlena congregation. Helen and I decided that I would visit by myself while she remained at home with the children. Since the mountain passes could receive a heavy snowpack at any time, I left as soon as feasible on the day after Thanksgiving.

Chapter Two: Utah

The mission at Toadlena was unfamiliar to me. All I knew was that it was located in the middle of the reservation against the foot of a mountain ridge. About thirty miles south of Shiprock, New Mexico, I had to turn off the main highway and take the final twelve miles to Toadlena. This was a new paved road, a relative rarity there, constructed by the government a few months earlier. Ahead of me was the Chuska Mountain Range. It seemed to take a long time to get close. When I got to the foot of the mountains, I saw the little village. And the first building I saw was a Mormon Church.

All over the village of about 250 residents there were trees. There was a government Bureau of Indian Affairs boarding school and housing for the teachers and other BIA employees. Next, on a short hill was an old trading post, and after that, turning left on the now dirt road, was the bright orange mission church that I was looking for. Up the hill from the church, spectacularly overlooking the village and the valley far to the east, was a large house. My correct guess was that it was the parsonage, and I drove to it. An older, small church building sat behind it. Besides this and the Mormon Church I had already passed, there were no other churches to be seen.

The questions were racing through my mind at this point: Could this possibly be our next home? Would we be able to adjust to living in this strange place? How would Helen be able to manage so far from a decent town with stores and medical care? How would our children make out in this area? All I could do was wonder.

Missionary Rich Kruis, the current pastor, was still living in the parsonage and he welcomed me into the house. Arrangements had been made that I would stay with them through the weekend. The beautiful view outside caught my attention immediately. One could see a hundred miles across the desert below. Behind the parsonage, on the mountain slope, was green forest. The house even had a grass lawn, a big garden, and fresh water from the church's own spring. There was a lot to talk about and see and I learned a lot of things that were important for me to know.

The mission in Toadlena was an old one, started back in 1910. At one point, one missionary, J.C. Kobes, had headed the mission

Chapter Two: Utah

for thirty-seven years. Kruis had been there for only two years, but was leaving for work in Michigan. The congregation was small. Some of the members had to travel a long distance to attend meetings at the church. During the summer months, one man would travel twelve miles to church on horseback. After the second worship service on Sundays, he would travel those same miles back to his home high up in the mountains. Some walked miles across the sandy desert to come to church. Several people drove the rough roads in their pickup trucks. There was no opportunity for employment other than a possible job at the boarding school where some worked as dormitory attendants or in the maintenance department. Almost all of the teachers were Whites (or "Anglos", as Whites were often called there) who had moved there from all over the nation. I was told that working among the Navajo here brought its share of communication problems. I would be working with an interpreter. About a third of the people could speak and understand English well. Another third knew it a little, while the final third knew no English at all. As for school, our children would have to attend a public school 12 miles away in Newcomb, be sent to the Christian boarding school in Rehoboth about eighty miles away, or be kept at home.

    As I laid in bed that night, it was hard to fall asleep. There was so much to think about. Besides all that, my feet were stone cold. It was obvious that the house had never been constructed with insulation between the walls. I could feel the cold wind blow right through the wall. The old coal furnace in the basement was in need of replacement. It could not heat the house adequately on cold days. It was clear to me that some improvements in the house would be necessary before we and our small children would ever be able to live there comfortably. Even the floors of the house were drafty, since there was no carpeting on the floors. I knew I would have to contact the Mission Board about these concerns.

    I also thought about the communication problem. Would those with limited English be able to understand me? It worried me so much that I asked the Lord that, if He wanted us to move to Toadlena, He would make it clear in church the next morning that I would be able to overcome that particular issue.

Chapter Two: Utah

I woke up to a foot of fresh snow outside. It did not keep the people from coming to church, for the small sanctuary was full. I gave a message on Matthew 7:7-14 where Jesus speaks about the wide and narrow roads. Immediately after the service, a lady came on the stage. In her hand was a tape recorder. She explained to me that she had taped my message so that she could interpret it all to her husband who was present at the service, but could not understand English. She said to me, "I will tell him everything you said, for I could understand every word you said."

As I walked to the back of the sanctuary to greet others, an older man came up to me and said, "I could understand you very well." It dawned on me then that these comments were an answer to the prayer of the night before. It was clear confirmation to me that the Lord wanted us to minister in Toadlena. If He would work out the problems with communication, then He would help us also to overcome other concerns.

That Sunday afternoon, it was time for me to return home. I had agreed to stop at the mission in Teec Nos Pos, Arizona and spend the night with that missionary family. There, I had a pleasant visit with Corwin and Esther Brummel and their family, with whom over time we would come to have an excellent friendship. Much of the way, the road was covered with a solid layer of ice. There was little snow removal equipment and the snow of the previous night was packed on the roads. This made driving almost impossible. Pickup trucks, commonplace on the reservation, found it especially difficult to scale the long, steep hills. It was interesting to watch one pickup roar past me to make it up a long hill ahead, but when I reached the top of the hill in my station wagon, which handled the ice well, I met the same pickup going in the opposite direction. It had completely spun around. No doubt living in a remote place like this would bring its interesting challenges.

I was happy to be home with my family. Helen was eager to get the report on my visit, and I was eager to share it with her. While we were talking that evening, we received a phone call from Rich Kruis in Toadlena. The members of the church had asked him to contact us on their behalf. They wanted us to know that they would really like us to come and help them. It reminded me

Chapter Two: Utah

of the apostle Paul at Troas, where he received a vision of a man in Macedonia saying to him, "Come over and help us." Even though an immediate reply seemed unnecessarily fast, we gave them the news that it appeared to us that the Lord wanted us to go there.

A few months later, representatives from the Christian Reformed Churches of Salt Lake City, Brigham City, and Ogden, plus the people of the Christian Indian Center met together for a farewell service. With a great outpouring of words of appreciation and well-wishing, they sent us off, closing the book on our Utah years and beginning the Reservation years that would constitute the vast bulk of our work in the mission field.

CHAPTER 3

Toadlena

MOVING IN

It was on January 21, 1969 that we moved from Salt Lake City to Toadlena, New Mexico. Arrangements had been made for us to stay at the Nataanii Nez Motel in Shiprock, about 45 miles northeast of Toadlena, for the first two nights since our furniture would not be arriving for two more days. Besides, the work of renovation done in the Toadlena parsonage was not quite finished.

The second day in Shiprock, we took a trip to Toadlena as a family. Helen and the children were eager to see our new home, as was I to see it all over again. There was a January thaw and it had rained. It was impossible to drive all the way up to the

Toadlena Christian Reformed Church

house on the hill because of all the mud. We decided to walk up the hill and sank up to our ankles in the ooze. Still, a group of dedicated workers from the Industrial Department for the Navajo mission were working feverishly to clean up and put the finishing touches on the work they had done.

The parsonage had received quite a makeover. There was a new heating system in the house as the old coal furnace in the basement had been taken out and replaced along with new hot water heating. The basement had been renovated and partially painted, as had been the main floor in the house. Carpeting was put down in the living room and dining room. The whole house felt warm and ready for us to settle in.

The following morning, we made a point of being back early, as we did not know when the moving van would be arriving. There were some initial concerns about whether the van would be able to get up the hill through all that mud. Fortunately, there had been a hard frost that night and the mud caused no problems. We were happy to see the van able to back up all the way up the hill to the house. Some men from the community who were aware of our moving in were waiting to be hired by the moving company and earn a few dollars that day. Our children were happy to see their favorite toys come out of the van and they wasted no time putting them to their intended use.

For the next few days we were busy settling in. No doubt about it—we were strangers in a strange land. From our windows was that wonderful view over the whole valley. It was all so big. We could see mesas and mountains a hundred miles away. To the north of us, the majestic Shiprock formation could be seen as it towered high above the desert floor. The house was very large with a total of 11 rooms, plus the full basement which included classroom space. Over the years, more and more rooms had been added. It seemed almost too big and too nice compared to the houses that others in the community had.

We thought of the missionary families that had lived in the parsonage before us. They were to be admired for their faithful years of service and how they had succeeded in gaining the confidence of the Navajo people. Rev. L.P. Brink, one of the first missionaries

Chapter Three: Toadlena

to the Navajo, spent a dozen years in Toadlena. People admired his knowledge of the Navajo language and he was known as "Dine' bik'is" (Friend of the Navajo). In 1925, Rev. Kobes began his 37-year tenure there. After that, Rev. J. Dykstra came, succeeded by missionary Rich Kruis. We were the fifth missionary couple to work in this place.

We would also have to get used to living in an area that was quite isolated from the rest of the world. The motel in Shiprock, which doesn't even exist anymore today, was the nearest one to Toadlena. Shopping would have to be done in Farmington, a larger city 30 miles beyond that, and taking a trip there took most of a day, especially when we would run all the errands which had accrued and purchased enough supplies for two weeks at a time. It was nice to know that the local trading post had some of the major food items for sale in case we would run out of something we needed. We would be doing our doctoring at Rehoboth, which was 80 miles to the south of us, but hopefully we would not need a doctor very often.

For the first few days, our neighbors looked us over carefully. They all seemed to know why we were there and were friendly to us. I shook a lot of hands and learned to say "yá'át'ééh" (hello) as a missionary was expected to do. We were called "bilagáana" (white man) and "éé' nishodi" (missionary). Some started to call me " éé' nishodi néz" (Tall Missionary) as they compared me with Rev. Kobes who was very short and known as "Little Missionary". Among those who spoke English, Helen and I became known as "Mr. and Mrs. K". A name as long as Klumpenhower was a big mouthful for most people, not unlike their language would be for us.

The Toadlena Church had a special welcome dinner planned for us and a large group of people from the area came together for the occasion. Everyone who was able brought food and participated in the event. The loose chairs in the sanctuary were moved aside for a long row of tables filled with different kinds of food that arrived in an assortment of containers. The meal consisted of fried mutton, mutton stew, fry bread, blue corn mush, boiled squash, yeast bread and ách'éé (fried sheep intestines). The latter was considered a delicacy and it reminded me of how we would say, in the older days,

Chapter Three: Toadlena

that we used to eat every part of a pig except for the squeal.

Our family was treated as if we were royalty as they seated us at a table while the rest of the people sat wherever there was a place to sit, even if that meant being on the floor. As the guests of honor, we were given plates and cups of good china, real silverware, and fancy napkins. Everyone else used paper plates, paper cups, and plasticware.

One of the leading men said a prayer of thanks to God before we were ready to eat. Our family was told to go through the line first where several ladies dished out the food and put it on our plates until the plates were heaping full. We all enjoyed it and I even had some food I had never eaten before such as the ách'éé and blue corn mush. It tasted fine to me, especially with a little salt. We learned that the people were not used to cooking food with salt but rather add the salt later. Nobody seemed to be bothered by the mutton stew that had cooled off a little too much on the way to church. The coffee that was consumed in great abundance was piping hot, however.

After the meal, when everyone was full, there were speeches from different people who shared their appreciation with us for coming to be their missionaries and they praised the Lord. After the singing of some Navajo and English songs, the people presented us with two Navajo rugs of the local Two Grey Hills variety which are widely famous for their natural colors and for their quality. Everyone seemed to know the weavers from the community who had put the masterpieces together. We were shown how one of the rugs was woven by a person who still adhered to the traditional religion as the weaver had made an intentional mistake in the design. It was explained that this was in order to express humility to the higher beings, while others said it was to let evil spirits escape. We also were given Navajo jewelry—brooches, rings, and necklaces—much of it decorated with turquoise stones. We were somewhat embarrassed with such an outpouring of generosity and appreciation. It was hard to know how to respond to such acts of kindness when they themselves had little of this world's riches.

Before everyone went home, we noticed that the older people and those with the greatest need were allowed to take home all the extra food that had been donated for the supper so that they could enjoy it the next day at home. Leftover food was not taken back home by those who had donated it.

Morris and Grace Nataani were members of Toadlena Church

A COMMUNITY IN POVERTY

A drive through the countryside revealed that our community was one with need. Most of the homes were small with just one or two rooms. Families were often quite large and I wondered how so many people could fit in such small houses. One look at the homes identified this area as one with great poverty, but it was also true that the people did not put a priority on keeping up a house as their value system was different from ours was. They treasured a good vehicle more than a good house. The favorable climate throughout most of the year made a big house less necessary anyway.

There was a definite lack of employment available, other than the few jobs at the schools where one could serve as a

Chapter Three: Toadlena

custodian or an aide in the classroom. Any job in the city was too far away, from here at least, and one needed dependable transportation to get there. Families did receive some commodity foods from the government, but that was not nearly enough to live on. The tribal government also tried to help somewhat by offering people ten-day work projects for which they were chosen by turn and for which they received wages. At these work projects, people were put to work helping to build new homes for mostly the elderly and the poorest families. Also, they helped by securing firewood and coal for those who were unable to help themselves. These work projects were good, but too short to have much long-term benefit.

Our church families were no exception. One day, I happened to notice a bag of flour in the church kitchen that apparently had been there for some time and was left unused. In order for it not to spoil, the idea came to me to give it to a needy family. I chose to deliver it to a particular family I knew was generally needy, although I was unaware of any particular need at the moment. When I arrived, I showed them my discovery as they looked on, stunned with wonderment. They then told me that this had been an answer to their prayers. They had just run out of food that day and prayed that the Lord would somehow supply them with food, such as a sack of flour from which they could make bread. You can imagine their joy at my arrival. Before I left, I asked them how they were going to be able to get by. The mother of the family just told me that they "lived by the Word of God." I'm not certain what exactly she meant by that, but it was evidence of a sustaining faith in their lives.

There were a number of people who had so little that it offered plenty of opportunity to show them charity. At home alone one day, while I was roasting a chicken in the oven, I noticed a neighbor walking past. He was a single man and one to be pitied for he could barely stake out a living. I felt that he needed to experience some generosity from me just as I had experienced in my many visits. I called to him and asked him if he would like to eat with me. He eagerly accepted my invitation and seated himself by me at the table. My guest could hardly control his excitement as the two of us finished the whole chicken. It felt good to me to have shared with him and I experienced that "It is more blessed to give than to receive."

Despite the poverty of the area, most families had multiple animals, particularly dogs, which ran around free to come and go as they pleased. They were particularly useful as watchdogs and with sheepherding. Most of these dogs never received any sort of special care and were generally expected to fend for themselves.

In the 1960's, the Johnson Administration in Washington D.C had decided to wage an all out war on poverty. Knowing that there were needs on the reservation, the government presented each household with a new sink and bathtub. This was of noble intent, but did not help many of the people since so few had running water in their homes. Apparently the government did not know how bad things really were. The sinks and bathtubs had no value to the people—except that a bathtub made a fine feeding trough for horses. In the meantime, all basic utilities—water, electricity, gas, phone service, etc.—were absent among a great number of homes in our area.

For those homes without running water, it had to be hauled home in barrels from the community wells that were located in different areas. Those fortunate to own a pickup truck used their vehicle for hauling the water. Others came to the community water supply with horse and wagon. Also, the necessary firewood and coal all had to be brought in. These were some of the chores that the men were expected to perform regularly. Families that lived farthest out in the countryside generally had no electricity, preventing them from having access to all modern appliances such as refrigerators, stoves, washers, and dryers—even if they could have afforded them.

One big help that all Navajo children who attended school on the reservation received annually was new clothing—a pair of shoes, a jacket, and other clothes given to them by the Navajo government. Any clothing not good enough to wear anymore was then gathered by the ladies and turned into quilts to keep the family members warm in the winter.

Some churches throughout the nation helped out the situation by sending barrels of good used clothing to churches on the reservation from where they could be distributed to those who needed them, including to us in Toadlena. These were delivered by some of the transport companies who volunteered to do so free of charge or as a donation to a worthy cause. Several days throughout the year we held clothing days at the church or in our basement when people from all over the area were invited to take what they needed. In order to guard against waste, we charged nickels and dimes for most of the items such as coats, pants, shirts, and shoes. Helen took on this excellent ministry of mercy, though it gave her even more responsibility than she had already taken on.

Most of the people at least managed to own a pickup truck. Usually these trucks were rather old and seemingly on their last legs, but the people kept them running as long as possible. Thanks to the dry climate, things did not rust too quickly. I have often been amazed at the mechanical ability the people possessed. Both men as well as women could often take an engine apart and have hundreds of parts lying all over the ground and then put the whole thing back together again. Old vehicles that were good only for the wrecking yard were usually kept for parts that could be used later, traded, or sold.

This was the condition in which most of the people in our area lived. We were certainly very blessed to be able to live in a parsonage that was equipped with many luxuries by comparison.

THE MIDDLE OF NOWHERE

One of the first things we had to deal with was getting Jack, now 5 years old, registered in kindergarten. The question was whether to send him to school at the mission school in Rehoboth, an hour and a half away, or the public school in Newcomb, just 10 miles away. We knew that the Rehoboth school was a fine school and the Christian education offered there was appealing. The problem was the 80 mile distance from home, and our little guy would have to either board at the school or with some friends in that area, being able to come home for a long weekend only once per month during the school year. On the other hand, the public school at Newcomb was close enough for him to be bused there and back each day. We opted for the latter as, in our opinion, not even the finest Christian boarding school can take the place of Christian parents and a Christian home.

Chapter Three: Toadlena

Newcomb Public School

Newcomb Elementary was still a big adjustment for our son, and not an easy one. The hardest thing for him was coping with being a minority, as there were only a few Anglo students that attended there. Although native children were generally nice to our boys at church and made friends with them, this was not always so at school where friendship with non-Navajos was an unpopular thing. Those children who tried to make friends with minority children were criticized by their peers and called "honky lovers". We made a point of talking about these problems at home and bringing out the good qualities in our children. In the meantime, we prayed with our children that the Lord would help them through hard times.

In order to help our boys make friends, we encouraged children from the church and community to come and play at our house. They had fun playing outside in our grassy yard, on the mountainside, and, occasionally, in the house, which worked out well—at least usually. In one instance, I had left some cans of grape juice out on a shelf intending them to be used the next morning

Chapter Three: Toadlena

for communion. When some of the visiting children noticed the cans, they apparently assumed that the juice was there for their benefit and promptly emptied the cans. The following Sunday morning, when we were going to celebrate communion at church, to my surprise, all the juice cans were empty. We had plenty of bread for communion, but not a drop of juice. It was not possible to get juice on a Sunday morning at the trading post for it was closed for business on Sundays. Besides that, they would not have had any grape juice available. We had no choice but to replace the grape juice with something else that was available to us. The best thing Helen and I could think of was mixing up some Kool-Aid with some added food coloring to darken it. We celebrated communion that Sunday as planned, telling no one of the substitution. In many places, using a mere drink mix for communion would be practically a sacrilege, but no one made any remarks about the strange juice we served.

Sometimes whole families came to make friends with us and visit us at the parsonage. We had to learn that when people came to visit, it did not necessarily mean that they had come to talk. Some were quite content to just sit and be with us without saying a lot. They enjoyed themselves looking at magazines or watching the children play. At times we went as far as to invite families over to the house for a meal, a token of friendship that was always appreciated.

At other times we served our visitors a cup of tea or coffee with a few cookies. It became evident that our guests were not familiar with our Midwestern custom of offering just a cookie snack, as in their culture they offered guests either a full meal or otherwise nothing. Some must have thought that our "meals" were pretty skimpy. Helen soon learned to make a point of telling visitors that what they were getting was just intended to be a little snack and nothing more.

Although this visiting took a lot of our time and sometimes disrupted our schedule and family life, they served the purpose of making friends and getting to know the people with whom we had come to work. Fortunately, it was quite acceptable for us to tell our guests that it was time for us to get back to work and that our visiting would have to come to an end.

Our fourth son, Mark, was born on May 19, 1970. For some time we had been concerned about how to get Helen to the hospital on time since the hospital was eighty miles from home. On top of that, Helen's time in labor tended to be short, and the babies tended to come earlier than expected.

The night before Helen began labor, an older couple from Denver, Colorado unexpectedly stopped by to visit with us and see the mission. Since there were no motels closer than the one in Shiprock, we invited the couple to spend the night at the parsonage. They accepted our offer unaware of the fact that they would become the babysitters for our children that night while Helen and I left for the hospital in the wee hours of the morning. As Helen was in delivery, the visitors found themselves serving the children breakfast in the morning and seeing to it that they got off to school. It seemed as if the Lord had planned all this in advance for us. As for ourselves, Helen and I had arrived at the hospital on time, but not a bit too early. Knowing that some missionaries lived a long distance away, the head nurse commented to Helen afterwards, "This is a good missionary baby. He gave you enough time to come in from a long distance."

Later that morning, our "Bible Woman" took over the care of the three older children as we had originally arranged. The CRC had a program in effect whereby people could volunteer to serve for one year to help on the mission field. These volunteers were expected to raise their own support that would cover their travel and living expenses. The Toadlena Church had a separate house for them to live in next door to the new church building.

It was a good program and resulted in some very dedicated people who came to help us. These volunteers were usually single ladies and were called the "Bible Women" on the reservation. Over the years, three different Bible Women served with us at Toadlena. They were a wonderful help with teaching the many Bible classes we taught at the boarding school. They also taught Bible classes for neighborhood children and for children in the public school. They took part in the ladies sewing circle and helped on days when we distributed clothing. Finally, they also helped with transportation

Chapter Three: Toadlena

and any other church activities. We owe these short-term missionaries many thanks for their faithful service.

With my job taking so much of my time and our being in such a remote location, I was thankful that Helen was brave enough to drive these distances when necessary. Helen did not particularly enjoy driving. She drove very carefully at all times, and rightly so. The roads were full of all kinds of hazards such as narrow bridges, deep dips, curves, drunken drivers and cattle. In this land without fences, cattle had a habit of standing on the road and, in particular, horses were notorious for doing so at night. Helen's cautiousness on the road did not go unnoticed. She was on her way to Farmington one day with the two youngest children in the back of our station wagon, driving slightly below the speed limit. A long row of trucks and other vehicles came behind her all waiting for an opportunity to pass. One of the children in the back was delighted, however, exclaiming, "What a long row of cars! And Mommy is the leader!"

The public school did give Helen the opportunity to do some substitute teaching whenever she wanted to do so. This provided her with an occasion to get out of the house now and then, which was good for her. I, myself, did not have such a need as I did a lot of visiting with people and frequently had meetings to attend.

Our children would also need special attention with me being busy and gone much of the time, especially in the evening. In order to correct the situation I took the older boys out fishing regularly, staying overnight whenever we went. After fishing, we built a small campfire and would fry the fish we caught on our little camp stove. It was a great time of sharing stories of my childhood with them and other experiences in life. The boys in turn would share what was going on in school and about their friends. We spent the night sleeping in the back of our station wagon where the boys always slept much better than their father did.

I also occasionally took the boys by turn for an evening in Farmington, an hour and a half away, just to visit together and to eat in the restaurant of their choosing, then to return home. Even Helen and I managed to get a babysitter now and then and spent an evening by ourselves. All of us have a need to get away from our daily routine and all our busyness. Three days of Christmas shopping each year in Albuquerque also allowed for time together and fun. So did our vacation time when we often traveled as a family across the country. These were enjoyable events that provided quality family time.

In the parsonage, we possessed one of the few telephones in the whole community. Naturally people came to our house to make use of it. The problem with this was that we often had to help place the calls as operating a telephone was still unfamiliar to many of them and their limited understanding of the English language made it hard for them to place a call. Besides that, Helen had to keep a record of all the calls in order to be able to collect the long distance fees after the phone bill had come. Still, it was a way of serving the people, and for that reason we continued the phone service for many years. Often, I was asked to deliver emergency messages to people in the countryside. This, too, was a way to serve them and to be "all things to all men".

Although it may seem like a small ministry, our openness to letting the community use the phone could be of critical importance to some. At the end of one evening meeting at church, a family came up to Helen and asked her to help them place a telephone call to the hospital in Gallup. Their infant daughter, Judy, was suffering from severe dysentery and had been taken to the hospital while the parents had to return home. Since I had left to transport some people home after the meeting, it was left to Helen to help them make contact with the hospital.

But to lend a helping hand was not all so easy that evening. The way from the church to the parsonage was uphill, the wind was terribly strong, and the driveway very muddy. She managed to go uphill very slowly carrying a baby in her arms trying to shield him from the cold wind while the older two children were hanging on to her coat so she could pull them up. A faulty heart valve did not help. Understandably, she was completely out of breath when she finally came to the house. Next, the telephone call had to be made, and the family needed her assistance since their ability to speak English was very limited, as was their understanding of it. It took a while to get all the information she needed from the parents before she could place the call. On the hospital's end of the call, they had to

Chapter Three: Toadlena

look for a nurse that would be able to converse with the parents in the Navajo language.

To top it all off, when the parents finally managed to receive news, it was that their little daughter was in serious condition and that it was not certain that she would live. Helen noticed the deep concern on the parent's faces and also spoke to the hospital staff to get as much information as possible. After the couple left for home, Helen put our children to bed and told them about the sick baby. She and the children prayed together that the Lord would heal the child. After several more days and more telephone calls to the hospital, the welcome news did come that the little child was beginning to improve, and we sent this message on to the family.

Several years later while teaching a Bible class at the local boarding school, Helen told her class how God had answered that prayer she and her sons had said for a little baby named Judy. Helen knew that Judy was one of the students in that class, and all the students were very impressed when this was revealed. It was a tremendous lesson on how the Lord answers prayer and how he has the power to help and heal.

Reaching the Lost

Not long after moving in, I was asked to attend a three-week training course in the Navajo language and culture at Cortez, Colorado. I took this course as this would provide me with some much-needed orientation to my work. Classes were held five days a week so that the students were able to spend the weekend with their families and in their churches. Although the study was very helpful to me, I was happy to be done after three weeks and be able to stay home again. Helen had been pretty lonely in the parsonage with no one to talk to except our small children. One of the ladies of the church, Lorraine Begay, began to make visits with Helen and made friends with her. For a number of years, Lorraine had been living off the reservation and was therefore able to relate to Helen's needs. This helped to lessen the feeling of isolation and the need for friends. Eventually Helen developed many other social contacts as well.

David and Katherine Yazzie, who lived about 10 miles out in the countryside, also came to make regular visits with us. They understood our need for encouragement and brought their Bibles when they came in order to share from God's Word with us. David did not speak English as he had not had the privilege of attending school. Katherine served as his interpreter, and in this way we were able to share and communicate together. For someone who was unschooled, we were impressed with David's knowledge of the Bible. With the help of his wife, he had taught himself to read the Navajo Bible translation and had memorized whole chapters of the Gospel of John. We always appreciated this family and their sharing

David and Katherine Yazzie

and praying with us. Their assistance was one certain way in which the Lord was to support us in our work. I found the job in Toadlena to be a daunting one where I could use such a willingness to serve, but I would ultimately need a full-time assistant.

In addition to church meetings, worship services, and the weekly Bible classes at the boarding school in Toadlena, I was also involved in the work of "campwork". Many of the people lived in groups of families known as camps. Campwork was the work of visiting these camps in order to present the gospel of Jesus. My predecessors had done this kind of visiting over the years and had

Chapter Three: Toadlena

gained good rapport. It seemed right to continue with it as it was a way of bringing the gospel to people who did not know it. This was mission work at its very core.

The Yazzies agreed to help with campwork and to serve as interpreters for me for some time. One full day each week, we took the church vehicle, or "mission truck", and went into the countryside together. When we came to a camp, we usually went to the house where the grandmother lived. We were invited into the homes to share our message with them. Often, the married daughters who lived in the other homes would also join in the meeting. We always shared a lesson from the Bible and brought out the teaching that Jesus is our Savior from sin. Time was spent in singing some Navajo gospel hymns together. Although the people were not familiar with these songs unless they attended church, they nevertheless enjoyed hearing them. We also spent time praying together, and as we left the home, we would leave an invitation to come to church.

Campwork did serve to bring people to faith in Christ. In most homes people listened with interest to the message we brought them. Most people thanked us for coming and gave an invitation to come again. Over the years this work also served to gain the people's trust in us.

Campwork, however fulfilling it could be, could have its difficulties too, even without the cultural barriers. You always wanted to make a good impression so that the people could readily see the love of Christ in you as you met with them. This did not always happen so easily. Once, while visiting with one couple, I noticed that the man of the house looked rather young compared to the lady present. Towards the end of our visit, we talked a while together and I made the mistake of asking the man, "How old is your mother?" Although this was a good question and normally well received by older people, this time the man looked at me seemingly puzzled why I had asked such a question. He answered me, "She is not my mother, but my wife." Despite awkward moments like this one, I generally enjoyed doing campwork.

There were jobs to be done that were less pleasant to do, however, and this included conducting funeral services. Many of the funeral services were for non-Christians who wanted some kind of a service for the dead. Since the medicine man was afraid of death and stayed away from dead people, the people looked to the Christian missionary to help them. At least this provided us with golden opportunities to bring the gospel message to people looking for hope.

Soon after our arrival at Toadlena, I was asked to officiate at a funeral for a single man who was not a Christian. I had not yet witnessed a funeral service on the reservation, so this was a new experience for me. In order to save the family some expense, I was asked to go to Farmington with the mission's pickup truck to bring the coffin to the funeral service. The man's relatives were very hesitant to do such a thing as they adhered to the traditional Navajo religion, and thus feared any close contact with death. The message that I shared at the service was from John 3:16. Although there was little comfort that I could give to the family of the deceased, I could share the hope and life there is when we receive Jesus as our Savior and Lord.

When the coffin was opened at the end of the service and people filed by to view the body, there was a surprise for me. Some of the men stuck bottles of wine and whiskey inside the coffin while some others put in a handful of money. I assumed that this was to help the deceased in the life to come. Undoubtedly, these were people who did not know the Lord.

At the gravesite, the coffin was gently lowered into the grave with three straps. Just as we were ready to cover it with dirt, a lady came running up to the grave. It was obvious to me that she had been drinking and she was unable to control her emotions. She was a sister of the deceased man and, because she had not been at the funeral service, she requested that she view the body one more time. The people adhered to her request and pulled the coffin out of the grave again. At last the coffin was buried and everyone threw a hand full of dirt on the coffin. I remember wondering what the purpose was for doing this. Perhaps to indicate a final farewell?

The grave was finally covered with a mound of soil and a large number of plastic flowers were laid on top. This was followed by a dinner for all at the home of one of the relatives. Everyone was there enjoying their food and friends, as did I. It felt somewhat strange for me to be the only white man present. It impressed me that their emotions could change so quickly from mourning back to something that might resemble normalcy. This first funeral served to show me how empty life is for those who do not know the gospel of Jesus and it increased my desire to share it with the people.

Not long after this, I was asked to take care of another funeral service, but this time for a newborn baby. It was doubly sad for me as I watched the child's parents, in dismay, not knowing where to turn for comfort. Again, I pointed the people to Jesus, explaining that it is He who is able to make life worth living in spite of all our hurts and problems. At this particular occasion, the coffin was stuffed with all the items a baby might need—diapers, formula, bottles, baby food, diaper pins. Apparently no one had asked themselves who would take care of the baby in the next life.

CAMPWORK

The Mission Board understood my need for a full-time assistant and interpreter. This led to the coming of Floyd Frank with whom I worked closely for eleven years at Toadlena. Floyd was from the community of Oak Springs, about sixty miles to the North. He had worked for years in a uranium mine. Some years after his conversion there was a call in all of the reservation churches for native people to help with mission work and to serve as lay preachers and interpreters. Floyd responded to the call quitting his job at the mine and being hired to assist us at Toadlena living in a third house on the property.

Campwork could now be increased with the additional help I had. Two full days each week, Floyd and I went visiting homes and together we covered an area of about twenty-five square miles. I enjoyed going on these visits together and we worked well as a team. I learned some of the basic techniques one should use when visiting with the traditional Navajo people as I watched Floyd. As a Navajo, he of course knew his own people well and knew the customs and culture. Among the things I learned from him were:

When you drive up to a Navajo home to make a visit, do not rush out of your vehicle, but take your time so that the people in the

Chapter Three: Toadlena

house have an opportunity to look you over and to prepare for your visit.

Do not bang on the door or knock hard for that might suggest that you are angry. On the contrary, tap the door lightly with your fingers.

Gary and Floyd doing campwork

Once inside the house, greet the people with a handshake going from the left to the right. You are not to grab someone's hand or pump the hand when greeting but touch the person's hand lightly.

It is also customary not to look a person into the eye when you greet him.

When indicating a certain direction, do not point with your finger but rather point with your lips.

Do not ask many questions and take time to think before you give an answer to a question addressed to you.

You must be careful not to speak too loudly, as only angry people and drunk people do that.

If you can learn to speak a few Navajo phrases, do so, for that will be appreciated by the older people. However, if you want to say something in Navajo, learn to use the correct pronunciation to show

Chapter Three: Toadlena

respect for the language.

Floyd and I made many visits together and some very interesting ones that may be shared. On one occasion, a young child let us inside the house of her great-grandmother. It was dark and very cold in the house. In one corner on the dirt floor was a pile of blankets. When the blankets began to move, we noticed that the great-grandmother was covered with the blankets trying to keep warm and possibly catch some sleep. She was stone deaf and had lost her eyesight. Floyd put a block of wood into the stove in order to warm up the room. There was no way for us to communicate with her other than to hold her hand. We sang a song and had prayer with her even though she did not understand us. As we were about to leave, she said in Navajo, "Thank you for coming to visit with me." Somehow she knew who we were and appreciated us coming.

Not long after, the same lady passed away and her relatives came to ask us to conduct a funeral service for her. No one knew her exact age but most of the people guessed her to be 111 years old. The only other thing we had really learned about her was that she had been a sheepherder all her life.

When we were called upon by our hosts to explain the message of salvation, I often used the example of our sinful self being like a man who had fallen into a deep pit. I explained that we were like such a man and needed help from God to save us, and that God, in his love, sent us Jesus who paid for our sins. He's like a man who throws us a rope to pull us out of our hopelessness. If we believe that Jesus paid for our sins on the cross, we are then saved.

This was the message we brought to another home where a mother and two grown daughters had invited us in. As we brought a Bible lesson, it was very obvious that the mother had great interest in what was taught as she was listening very intently. As I was using this man-in-a-pit illustration, the mother interrupted me and said excitedly, "I know that you are telling the truth because I had a dream that was just like you explained. In my dream I was stuck in a deep pit and unable to get out. Then I saw Jesus come to me and He pulled me out." Then she said that she wanted to be a Christian and commit her life to the Lord, but that she was not able to become a Christian. She said, "I have never attended school and cannot read this book and cannot memorize what it says." She was holding in her hands an old catechism book that someone had given her years earlier. She had concluded that unless you memorize the whole catechism, a person cannot become a Christian. We were happy to be able to correct her and to let her know that a person becomes a Christian and receives salvation simply when he accepts Jesus as his Savior and Lord.

Not long after this, the mother was baptized at our church. She died a year later of complications caused by diabetes, but left in full confidence of her salvation. Soon after this, one of the daughters requested that we instruct her in her mother's new faith. She also committed her life to the Lord and became a faithful member of the church.

About ten miles into the countryside and far off the paved road lived another family that asked us to teach them the Christian faith. Floyd and I therefore made a regular visit at their home one evening

Harvesting corn

each week for several months. While we were having a lesson with them one night, the wind began to blow outside. The stovepipe rattled loudly and we could hear the sand as it blew against the house. It was important that we leave as soon as possible before it would become impossible to see the road due to the dust. We managed to find our way back even though at times we could barely see where we were going.

Suddenly some black animal was walking directly in front of our vehicle. We came to a stop before we hit it. I thought that it must be a dog, but soon we saw that it was a small, black lamb that had apparently gotten separated from its mother that day. Despite the terrible conditions outside, we got out, picked it up, and took it home where it was kept in a cardboard box next to the furnace for the night. A lonely lamb like that would almost surely be killed by a hungry coyote or fox, if not by the violent weather. In finding it, we had most likely saved its life.

The following morning we returned to that area determined to find the owners of the lamb and to return it. We found the owners and they were delighted to have their lamb back. The little animal, in turn, was happy to be reunited with its mother and the other sheep. There were Bible lessons here to be learned and I determined that we would return to this family some day and, the Lord willing, to tell the story from Luke 15 where Jesus told about a shepherd and a lost sheep. At a more convenient time we did just that, and, though the family responded with gratitude, they never showed further interest in the Lord. They were left with a good reminder of the love of God for the lost and this would hopefully stay with them for a long time.

Almost every time we went visiting, we were reminded of how so many people are in great need of a Savior. One family we visited told us that their father had died and now they wished for us to hold a funeral service for him, even though they adhered to the traditional religion of the Navajo. We conducted a service as requested and afterwards joined the family for the burial not far from his home on the side of a large hill. As the coffin was lowered into the grave, I noticed the family members laying a beautiful new saddle on it, which they wanted buried also. As I had already seen before, this was not altogether to be unexpected. What happened next, though, I did not expect. From behind the hill came the loud, unnatural neighing of a horse. A group of men had just killed the man's favorite horse by clobbering it in the forehead with an ax, thereby making it possible, according to their beliefs, for horse and rider to be together in the hereafter. This slaughter was a heartbreaking thing to witness. I comforted myself with the knowledge that Jesus was able to penetrate that spiritual blindness with the truth of the gospel.

We made regular visits with another family where the mother had become a believer and joined the church, but her husband avoided us as much as he possibly could. Whenever we came into the house through the front door, he would escape through the back door. This went on for a few years.

One day when we returned to visit, the husband was sitting on the bed with the intention of listening to our Bible lesson. He explained why his attitude had changed and why he suddenly had an interest in the Word of God: There had been no rain showers that summer and everything he had planted was drying up due to the lack of moisture. This included the small patch of alfalfa clover from which he hoped to harvest a few bales of hay for his horse and sheep. As he stood by his field he bowed his head and prayed a prayer to Jesus and said, "If you send water for my land then I will serve you". Soon thereafter there was a heavy rain shower on top of the mountain about ten miles from his home. The water rushed down the mountain arroyo eventually flowing directly past his alfalfa field so that he was able to irrigate his land and thus save his crop. Thereafter he committed his life to Jesus and, after some more instruction, he also joined the membership of the church. The Lord was continuing to add gems for His crown, one by one.

As we made visits over the years, the generosity of the people continually impressed me. I had learned earlier that Native Americans traditionally have always shown generosity to others as they measured success not by how many goods they possessed but by how much they could share with others. This is a fine Christian concept and a good tradition, but one that is, unfortunately, being lost today.

There were a number of times when we were offered food as we visited. I much preferred it when we got hot mutton ribs, especially with a piece of frybread, but often it, along with a piece of squash, would be cold—neither foods being my favorites without being

Chapter Three: Toadlena

heated up. We always accepted it gratefully, though I must confess that when one generous man offered me a cooked sheep eye, rather than just eat it politely, I told him kindly that it would be better for him to eat it as this was new to me. He happily ate it himself, along with some sheep brain.

We were often offered black coffee as well when we visited the camps. Again, we appreciated the people's generosity and generally took whatever was offered to us. Once, however, as we met outside with a family, the coffee we were given was so incredibly strong that it was impossible for me to drink it. Not willing to embarrass our hosts, I waited for an opportunity to pour the contents on the ground behind me while no one was looking. It took some patience, but I managed to do as planned without being noticed—or so I thought. Unfortunately, the family dog had been sniffing about for some morsels, and the moment I had tossed the coffee out behind me, he came over to see what I had thrown out. Perhaps the family hadn't noticed its particular interest in my area, for no one said anything about it. I decided I had made a wise decision, though, especially as Floyd, who had been more daring, was complaining of a stomachache later that day.

During the summer months, most of the people who owned some cattle or sheep left the hot, dry desert and moved to their summer camp high on the mountain. On the mountain it was cool and very pleasant and there were trees and grass for the cattle. The people lived in very simple log cabins but spent a lot of time sitting around the outdoor fireplace where they cooked food and boiled coffee. Floyd and I were well received whenever we came to visit them. We would be invited to sit with them, not only to share the gospel, but also to give an update on the local and national news.

At one of the homes, I was sitting outside on the side of a bed patiently listening to Floyd's lengthy interpretation of the little devotion I had given, followed by a prayer. In the middle of his prayer, I felt something suddenly poke out right between my legs from underneath me. I nearly jumped right up off the bed. A large tom turkey had apparently been sitting under there the whole time without my knowledge and decided on that particular moment to get up. It maneuvered its way out from under the bed and trotted on its way. My concentration on the prayer was slightly interrupted, to say the least. At least I wasn't the one speaking.

It shouldn't be surprising that these visits often came with humorous moments, especially considering the cross-cultural nature of the job. It was also common for the camp animals, which often ran unfettered around camp, to be the stars in these stories.

In fact, once, when we were several hundred feet away from the house where we had made a visit, I happened to look back through the side mirror of our mission vehicle. The lady of the house was running after us and frantically waving her arms. Floyd stopped the truck and we both got out wondering what might be the lady's problem. Then we heard a noise in the back of the truck. One of her goats had jumped in the back and was hitching a ride with us. Although we had a camper shell on the back of the truck, there was no door to it, so the goat managed to jump in. We were sure glad we hadn't made it all the way home without noticing our stowaway. What a surprise that would have been!

Yet another time we were driving along the dirt roads and kept on hearing a cat's meow. We figured that once again we had a stowaway, as cats are certainly prone to making their resting spots on or in warm vehicles. We stopped to search for it, looking in all the probable locations—under the hood, behind the seats (we had left our windows open), in the back of the truck—but we found nothing. We shrugged our shoulders and figured we had just better go on. As we continued on our way, sure enough, there was that cat mewing anxiously again. Again we stopped and made another thorough search, again to no avail. Where could that noise be coming from? We couldn't both be imagining it, could we? A third time we continued, and a third time we heard it. We stopped the truck immediately. This time we were determined. We would find that cat here and now, even if we had to take the truck apart. Finally, Floyd thought to actually crawl underneath the truck where he found the cat clenched onto the rear axle. I can hardly imagine the sort of ride it had endured just holding on for dear life.

We retrieved the cat, turned around, and went back to the last house where we'd visited. The moment we stopped by the house the cat got out and ran into the house. When we explained to the people why we had returned, the whole family burst out laughing and explained that their cat did that all the time.

During the summer, Floyd and I would spend one full day each week making visits with people up the mountain. We both enjoyed being up there and away from the summer heat. We would take a sack lunch along and a thermos of coffee. At lunch time, we often sat by a mountain well where we could freshen up and drink the cool mountain spring water. Sometimes we rested under the tall Ponderosa pine trees.

Floyd would, in these times, tell me stories of his boyhood years when he would spend the whole summer away from home and with his grandfather herding sheep up the mountain. They would live on mutton, tortillas and coffee. At times they had to confront bears that tried to steal the sheep and had to scare them away by rattling an old coffee can with some stones inside. This and the loud barking of the sheep dogs would be enough to scare the bears away.

As we drove along a mountain trail one day, we noticed a large pine tree lying on the ground next to us. It had been split into two clean halves from top to bottom as a result of a lightning strike. Most people did not dare touch it or even come close to it out of fear that this would bring them some sort of harm. Floyd was not afraid of such superstition, however. He later returned to the tree, cut it into sections and hauled it piece by piece to our camp shelter where he made long tables to be used when food was served at our camp meetings.

WORSHIP AND OUTREACH

Sundays were always our big day of the week. Before church in the mornings there was a large class of children to teach at the boarding school. During this time, Floyd went to pick up people for church who had no transportation. People were instructed to come to the main roads where they would be picked up and returned after the church service. We began church services as much as possible on time. Many of our people were not accustomed to going by

Chapter Three: Toadlena

the clock and preferred to come at their own time or whenever convenient. This was something to get used to for people like Helen and myself who were brought up with the teaching that we needed to be prompt when attending worship services.

The service always began by a time of singing. If there was no one to play the piano, as was often the case, we sang a cappella and were led by a few families that were asked to serve as song leaders. Singing songs was a popular thing to do, especially when we sang in the Navajo language, even though that presented some difficulties as very few people knew how to read their own language. Also, when the Navajo language is put to a tune, it loses much of its meaning and we would sometimes read the song before singing it so it could be understood better. Following a time of prayer and greeting, there would be a sermon. The message was preached in the English language, but translated into Navajo by paragraph or, sometimes, line by line. There was usually an opportunity somewhere in the service for a few people to share a testimony of God's grace in their lives or to sing a hymn for the congregation. A second service on Sundays was held later that day at Newcomb.

The length of our services was also something to become accustomed to since we met for about two hours, and that was still

Bible class at Toadlena Boarding School

Chapter Three: Toadlena

followed with an hour of Sunday school for everyone. In addition, it was important to socialize with each other after the Sunday school hour and have some coffee. The length of time did not seem to bother many people as they had come from a long distance and were expecting a full service that was worthy of their time.

We admired the fact that the people were able to relax when they came to worship. It was not stoic or stodgy as churches back East tended to be, but rather it was normal to laugh together during our worship. With our long services, it was perfectly acceptable to walk out in the middle of a service for a short break and then to come back in. These things were never done in churches where I had been brought up. Of course, those churches had never been in a place quite like this.

One Sunday when all the windows were opened wide due to the heat, a horse which had wandered off stuck its head through an open window to see what was going on inside. This, as you can imagine, brought a sudden roar from the worshippers.

Our people put a lot of value in prayer at a worship service. They appreciated a time of sharing prayer needs at Sunday services and the midweek prayer meetings. It was interesting that they had no problem with leading in a prayer in public, whereas in our home churches back east, some people were very hesitant to do so and felt uncomfortable leading in a prayer. In our Navajo churches we put a lot of emphasis on prayer for this was an area in which the churches were strong.

Special days—particularly in and around holidays—were often observed, and with some notable differences. An Easter service was held at sunrise outdoors on the east side of a large mesa about two miles down the road from our church. We would build a fire and sit around it in folding chairs as we waited for the sun to appear above the horizon to begin the service. We had a wonderful view over the whole valley and could see people coming in their vehicles from all directions. Here in the beauty of God's creation, we could remember his special love for us in a particularly powerful way.

During the Christmas season, a great many bags of peanuts and candy were prepared for all the children at the boarding school. Sometimes the bags included a small toy for the children also. Both young and old received a bag with goodies at church also. This was a real treat and was made possible with some gift money that was sent for the occasion by individuals or societies from sponsoring churches. A Christmas program each year was very popular and brought in several visitors from the community who did not come at other times.

It was not uncommon for a nativity play to be performed. These were, of course, not even remotely professional performances, nor was that the intent of them. It was a unique way of sharing the Gospel, and a fun one—perhaps more so because of its amateur nature. One year, a Bible class of ours acted out the story of the wise men. Some of the boys served as camels while others were wise men who came into the sanctuary riding their camel. Unfortunately for one of the wise men, his camel was not watching where he was going as he mistakenly went off track and crawled under one of the tables in front of the church knocking the helpless rider to the floor. Regardless, these services were a special occasion every year that helped make the Christmas season something to be treasured.

A Sunday School class in Toadlena Church

On New Year's Eve, we always held a Watchnight service where people played games together starting at around 9:00 PM, and then, at 11:00, we would gather by candlelight for a service where people were called to rededicate themselves and the upcoming year to the Lord. The church bell was rung at the close of the service at midnight when the people would go home—sometimes with me taking those without rides—which made for a long day for me, but one without regrets.

The church at Toadlena organized a regular evangelism event simply called "camp meeting." This meeting was usually held during the fall in an outdoor shelter near the church. There was an abundance of food served at these meetings and sheep and goats were donated and butchered right by the camp shelter. Young and old came to enjoy the fried mutton, mutton stew and fry bread. The meetings lasted for about three days and much time was spent listening to a guest speaker who brought evangelistic messages. Although the main purpose for these meetings was to serve as an outreach to the non-Christian community, it was certainly also a social event where Christians from different churches around the area met for fellowship. People sang Christian hymns and shared many testimonies of how the Lord had brought them to faith or how the Lord had blessed them.

These meetings often attracted a good number of people, but the smell of food also brought a pack of neighborhood dogs that were constantly in search for something to eat. They were not unlike the seekers who came looking for spiritual food. One of the dogs was walking around with a very crooked back and a pitiful sight, but the speaker for the meeting used it to explain an important point of his message. He commented, "That dog needs an alignment job just like some people who have wandered away from the Lord."

The Lord used these camp meetings as one way of bringing people to faith in Him. One year a teenage girl came forward to dedicate her life to Jesus. She explained that, now that she was a Christian, she would search for a place to live other than with her parents and siblings. Whether her family would be rejecting her as a Christian or whether she refused to live in an ungodly environment, we do not know. The young lady asked a neighboring family to take her in but that was not a good situation for her. Helen and I decided to take her into our family for a while to help her and give her a morale boost and give her some much needed Christian teaching. She accepted our offer gratefully and, so, for the next few months we had a big sister in our household besides our four sons. It was a big adjustment for this young lady to live with us at our home and this had its difficulties for her. After some time, she decided to return to her parents. We noticed after that an apparent falling away from the Lord, but a few years later she did return as a faithful believer. We will always remember her singing in her bedroom while she lived with us. One big desire she had was to own a dress that she could wear to church on Sundays. We bought her a pretty new dress and presented it to her on her sixteenth birthday.

Another method of outreach into the community was a Bible conference held up the mountain for 10 days during the summer known as "Cottonwood Pass." These meetings were held in conjunction with the other Christian Reformed churches on the reservation. Many families camped at that conference while others commuted back and forth each day. We personally enjoyed them and took part in them as we camped there as a family. It was a time for spiritual refreshment and fellowship among Christians.

Our children also enjoyed this conference every year. Besides the natural lure of wilderness camping for them, they enjoyed the opportunity to run around and play in the mountain scenery, or just get lost in its beauty. It was a welcome relief from the hot desert floor below them. Our children enjoyed the children's and youth activities offered there, and they made a number of friends. It was always something that we looked forward to each year.

It was good that our native leaders did much of the speaking at these conferences. It was one more way in which they were taking the reins of the work of leading their own people in being followers of God. One of the speakers at the conference made a remark that I will always remember. He pointed to all the towering pines and said, "These are all fingers that point straight up to their Great Provider." To this day whenever I walk through a pine forest I am reminded of this truth as I now see them as fingers to remind me of my wonderful Creator and Provider.

Chapter Three: Toadlena

THE EXPANSION OF THE GOSPEL MESSAGE

A young couple came to visit us one day at our home. They knew both of us, but we did not remember them until they

Dean Slim and Jim Klumpenhower at Cottonwood Pass Bible Conference, July 1977.

identified themselves as former students of Intermountain School in Brigham City, Utah. They had been members of the choir I used to lead. Later on, after graduating from school, they both came to faith in Jesus. The couple was living in Borrego Pass, an area that was 100 miles east of us. Knowing that we were living in Toadlena, they decided to visit and share with us some of their needs. They told of their desire to begin a Christian church in their home area where there was no church and asked for some advice and hopefully receive encouragement. We prayed with them and asked the Lord to bless their efforts and I gave them a copy of a few books that I thought might be helpful to them, including *Halley's Handbook of the Bible*.

Some years later, when I was attending a meeting of missionaries from a variety of Christian denominations, a missionary came to me and said, "As a result of your plowing in the community of Borrego Pass, there is now a Christian church there."

Chapter Three: Toadlena

He shared with me how the Lord had richly blessed the young couple that had been visiting with us and that the believers had put up their own church building. It was wonderful to learn how our visit had impacted an entire community, as well as see this belated fruit from our work during our Brigham City days. To the best of our knowledge, the couple is still ministering there for the Lord Jesus today. Only God knows how many other lives have somehow been touched by any of us who have given themselves to the work of the Lord.

Not an inch to spare! Old Toadlena Church building is moved to Beclabito, NM.

Over the years we could see that the church of Jesus was expanding on the reservation. Many independent church groups began to appear in many places. These did help to spread the gospel, but sometimes they also did damage to God's work by competing with the existing churches and by being unnecessarily critical of them. Often their leaders were not well trained in the Word of God and preached without being properly tested and with little accountability. These small church groups usually became family churches composed mostly of one clan where members of other clans did not feel welcome. Their lack of organization also caused many disagreements among the adherents. The advantage of these small groups was in the fact that they were instantly self-governing and self-supporting while the churches such as ours continued to need assistance from outside sources.

The growth of the Christian church among the Navajo was very slow during the first fifty years. There were a number of reasons for that. Christianity was often seen as strictly a white man's religion and, naturally, many of the Navajo were reluctant to give up their Navajo identity in order to join it. It was erroneously believed by many of them that a person could not be a Christian and a Navajo at the same time. Missionaries were often at fault, however, as they brought their system of church government which was foreign to the people along with them as they preached the Gospel.

Historical reasons also made it hard to put trust in the white man and the Christian message he brought. Throughout history, the Navajos as well as other Native Americans had experienced broken treaties and the stealing of the land, and such evil treatment was still on people's minds. The fact that the Navajo had been forced off their land during the 1860's by the federal government was still understandably very much a sore spot to them.

A large number of non-Navajo people who were employed in the reservation schools as teachers or at the hospitals did not exemplify a Christian lifestyle, even though they professed to be Christians. They seldom attended church services and seemed to worship sports and pleasure more than the Lord. Their nominal faith also made Christianity seem less attractive to the Navajo as it demonstrated no advantage over their own traditional beliefs which had been passed on from generation to generation.

In spite of these negatives, the Lord has continually been building His church among the Navajo. It is estimated that today one-tenth of the Navajo population is embracing the Christian faith. This is quite remarkable, even though it is a small minority of the people. The pace of church growth has greatly increased since the nineteen-fifties and many larger church buildings were built, including at Toadlena. The first building could seat no more than forty people, which had sufficed for fifty years until the present building, which holds 150 people, was constructed in 1968. It seemed as if we had suddenly reached a period of harvesting souls instead of just plowing and planting and sowing the seed.

A few years after the new church building was constructed and the old building was no longer needed, it was decided to donate the old building to a small group of believers in Beclabito, NM who had no building. The old church bell was taken out of the tower before the building was moved, since there were plans to construct a new bell tower for it in the future. It continued then, upon completion of the new tower, that on Sunday mornings the bell could be heard for many miles across the desert as it reminded people to come and worship the Lord.

BRINGERS OF ANOTHER GOSPEL

Rich Kruis, my predecessor, had put up a wooden box by the community water well. This box was kept full of Christian reading materials, including leftover Sunday school papers which children could take home while the family was getting their water. It was a good idea which we continued and people made good use of it by taking home whatever we put in the box. One day, however, I noticed the town's two Mormon missionaries empty the box of all its contents and take off with them. Later, we learned that they distributed our materials to families in the community as an attempt to assure them that Mormons are Christians and teach the same as Christian churches teach, only a little better. We came to see them as the bringers of another gospel that had no need for the Jesus we preached. They came to disrupt our work and to work against us.

Mormon missionaries on the reservation were in some ways better equipped to serve on the reservation. They were well-trained in Navajo language and were able to converse with the Navajo people better than most Christian Missionaries were. Their message of high moral standards and high family values was appealing. Yet, their message was not the gospel of Jesus, but rather that of salvation through the Mormon church—through man's own efforts instead of God's grace.

They were masters at deception, using Christian terminology but not accepting its meaning. One time, for example, after I heard

Chapter Three: Toadlena

one of their bishops lead in a prayer, I asked why he addressed God as "Eternal" and referred to the "Holy Trinity", since they do not really believe in either of these things. His response was that these were merely names for God and nothing more, just as we use "Lord" and "Savior" as names for Him.

We had also noticed that Mormon missionaries were going house to house on the reservation carrying a Bible, even though the Bible is least in importance among the four Mormon books they consider collectively as "the Scriptures". They were well aware that their Book of Mormon had little clout among the Navajo compared to that of the Bible. After people joined their church, the Bible was put aside, and the people were then given strictly Mormon teaching.

Their methods of reaching the community could be very clever and effective. The Mormon church encouraged their people to buy up all the trading posts on the reservation wherever possible. Since these were often the only possible places anywhere nearby where one might get basic necessities, this gave them great access to the people and a certain hold on them, providing Mormons an upper hand within the community.

At the boarding school, parents could sign up their children to receive religious instruction from either us at the Christian Reformed mission or from the Mormons, not unlike the system we had at Brigham City's Intermountain School. The traders were known to sometimes put pressure on the people to sign up their children as Mormon so that they would then be instructed in the Mormon faith instead. Still other traders pressured parents to sign up their children for the Mormon placement program in Utah where their children would be baptized and instructed in the Mormon faith immediately. It was hard to believe that such tactics were supported by leaders at Temple Square in Salt Lake City, by a church so eager to leave a good impression in the world.

The Mormon church had requested permission to put up a church building in Sheep Springs, about 20 miles to the southeast of Toadlena, but the request was denied by the local chapter, the reservation's smallest administrative districts. The Mormon trader at the trading post, however, put up a special building in his back yard. This building was mainly a gymnasium with hot showers. This was an effective draw to community youth, offering sports activities and shower facilities which few had access to normally. Of course, one would have to sign up as members of the Mormon church in order to take advantage of such facilities.

NEWCOMB

Some major changes were also taking place in Newcomb with our church and also at the public school where our children were attending. The school was expanding rapidly and was adding more classrooms,

A new church building at Newcomb under construction.

a large gymnasium, and more housing for teachers. We made a point of praying that the Lord would send more Christian teachers to that school who could be influential in helping us point people to the Lord. Such teachers could also be a real support to our church as they worshipped with us. The Lord answered our prayers and provided the school at Newcomb with a Christian principal and his family plus four other Christian families along with five single Christian teachers.

Many of these people joined us in worship on Sundays at Toadlena and were a wonderful asset to the church. They purchased Christian comic books that children could read after school hours or

Chapter Three: Toadlena

take home. They spent time counseling children when the children shared their problems with them after school hours. These teachers discovered a wonderful ministry in God's kingdom.

The community of believers in Newcomb soon found itself in need of a new place to worship. For years, a small group met for worship in an old school house on Sunday afternoons. The facility was in poor condition and the roof was very leaky. One winter, after a snowstorm, the melted snow found its way through the roof and into the meeting room. When we came for worship the following Sunday, all the chairs were covered with a thick layer of ice and so was the heating stove in the middle of the room. Each chair was frozen solid into the ice on the floor. The people worshipped anyway, just as at other times, and fired up the wood stove with some blocks of wood and some coal. The room turned into a steam bath that Sunday.

Not long thereafter we were informed that the building was condemned and worship would have to be discontinued in it. The worshipers met together and decided to request a church site from the community and eventually put up a building on that land. The Mission Board assured them that the CRC would put up a trailer in which the people could meet once the land site had been approved. At the local chapter meeting the request for the church site was discussed. Unlike the situation in Sheep Springs with the Mormons, this proposal passed with a unanimous vote from the community of 105 - 0. The one acre piece of land was fenced off, and soon we received the gift of a long, narrow trailer shell that was ready for use.

The Newcomb community was informed that the new structure was there for their benefit. We made a point of inviting the whole community for a dedication service and time of feasting together. The service featured the typical abundance that such meetings would produce as most families brought all kinds of food for the occasion. Before the dedication took place, however, we had already used it for a funeral service for a member of the community, a fact which demonstrated its importance already. When the dedication service was held, it seemed as if the whole community had come to celebrate. The trailer was packed with people and still many others were left outside without a seat. The doors were left open for the service so that those outside could also hear, as well as to provide

Chapter Three: Toadlena

fresh air for those inside.

Even better for me was the following Sunday when many of these same people returned for worship who had not done so previously. That trailer building remained full of people on Sundays and people came to faith in Jesus. One Good Friday evening, twenty-five people were baptized together, and all except for one couple were from the Newcomb community.

About a year later, the people began to make plans for a larger and a more permanent building. There was no money to pay for such an undertaking and to borrow funds and put the group in heavy debt was not wise. But the Lord would have his way of helping and of answering the people's prayers.

The new church at Newcomb is completed. On the right is the former church (trailer).

The men spent several days cutting logs out of the forest on the mountain and hauling them down. After that, both men and women helped in the sticky job of peeling every log so these could dry properly and eventually be used as rafters for the roof. When we were told that we could have access to much of the lumber from the old hospital at Rehoboth that was being torn down, our people got together with their pickup trucks and brought much of that lumber into the building site also. Next came the digging of a foundation which was all done by hand. This was hard work as the ground was very dry and hard. This, too, was completed and all without any expense. Unfortunately, there came an unforeseen setback. A heavy cloudburst washed all the hard work under water and all was filled with heavy mud. We overcame this discouragement together, digging out a foundation for the second time.

The highway that ran through Newcomb was being renovated at that time. Some of the men from the community found employment by working for the construction company. One of the local men lost his life to a tragic work accident, and I was asked to conduct the funeral. After the service, the construction foreman came to me to share some words of appreciation. He had heard of our plans to put up a church building at Newcomb and of the difficulties we had encountered. He then suggested that we accept a helping hand from the company. He said to me, "We're building a new bridge for the highway in Newcomb. Why don't I order some extra concrete and use that to pour all the fittings for your foundation? And I'll send one of my men with a bulldozer to level that whole church property for you."

Even with this and other help, it all together took ten years to complete the building at Newcomb, a project that was not completed until long after my time in Toadlena had ended. Little by little people donated as they were able the necessary cinder blocks and other building materials. Some dedicated volunteer workers who served at Rehoboth pitched in by lending their help. Even one family from Portland, Oregon with carpentry experience came out to assist us.

The end result of all this work is a fine church building that is free from debt. The church group is headed today by two of their own lay leaders who run the worship services and preach the gospel, including David Yazzie who used to help me at Toadlena. The church is functioning as a small indigenous church and is known as Bizteezáhí (Newcomb) Christian Reformed Church.

LIFE AS A MISSIONARY FAMILY

Life on the reservation was not all work, of course. The church and parsonage were located on several acres of land which allowed

Chapter Three: Toadlena

Our family photo, 1976; sons, left to right: Jim, Jack, David, Mark.

for plenty of space for me to engage in two of my favorite hobbies: Gardening and raising birds. In particular, I was generally in the possession of a number of chickens and pigeons, the former of which were kept for eggs and the latter of which I raised for pure enjoyment and sold at no profit to others who wished to raise them themselves. Unlike many people, my animals were kept cooped up, but that didn't always keep the dogs, hawks, or other predators running wild in the area from coming in for a convenient dinner.

I had noticed that over a period of several days one summer that some of my chickens had gone missing. When one day our baby chicks were calling for their mother and mother hen had disappeared, I decided that something needed to be done. "It's probably a bobcat", I said to myself.

I told Floyd about my problem and he came over immediately to see for himself. I knew that his long experience with mountain animals might help him identify my culprit. He told after looking over the situation, "It is not a bobcat, but a dog. It scaled the fence over there and went up the mountain with the hen." Indeed, there was one dog track by the fence and a few small feathers that gave it

Chapter Three: Toadlena

away. We decided to track the dog up the side of the mountain until we found it. Floyd led the way displaying an amazing ability to track an animal. Here and there he saw evidence that the dog had been there, even though I saw nothing to speak of out of the ordinary. After some time we saw another chicken feather on our trail and it proved that we were hot on the trail. Sure enough, we came to the edge of a deep ravine, and as Floyd looked into the ravine he quietly motioned to me to come and see. At the bottom of the ravine was the dog. Apparently the hen had gotten away and was perched on a branch just outside of reach. We were able to rescue the hen and return it to the chicks.

We identified the dog as one that belonged to one of our neighbors. When the owners of the dog heard what had happened, they bought our family two fryers to make up for those that had been stolen. They also brought the dog on a leash to contain him and then explained that the dog was not good and was causing problems. They asked us to shoot it. Inasmuch as a pest like that was not good for the community, Floyd did as we were asked, so ending the life of my chicken thief.

I encountered a different kind of thief at the Shiprock hospital where I had taken a sick woman in the middle of the night. While waiting for the doctor's prognosis, someone must have siphoned the gasoline out of my car. As I began to head for home at 2:00 AM, I noticed immediately that the fuel gage indicated that the tank was almost empty. This was bad news for there was no open gas station anywhere in the area. I would either have to wait until daybreak when a station would open for business or head for home and chance running out of gas in the middle of nowhere. I decided to do the latter and pray as I went, hoping I could make it the whole 45 miles back where I had a large can of gasoline in reserve for emergency situations. At a speed of 40 miles per hour I hoped to conserve enough fuel to get at least close to home. The vehicle stalled about one mile from home as the last few miles were uphill and took more fuel than was in the tank. I walked home, and after waking Helen from her sleep, we returned to the car in the mission truck and were able to bring it home. There was no doubt in my mind that a gasoline thief was worse than a chicken thief.

Chapter Three: Toadlena

Occasionally I would have an opportunity to relive some of my boyhood days on the farm by butchering our own animals for meat. One of Floyd's relatives who lived in Shiprock had raised two pigs and wanted to sell them. Knowing that our family ate pork, we were offered the pigs for $30 each. The pigs had been outside all year and fed on corn and alfalfa, weighing about 300 pounds each. We made a deal and agreed on a day to butcher them. Floyd volunteered his help and I appreciated that as he knew more about how to butcher an animal than I did. I was thankful for what I had learned as a young boy watching pigs being butchered by my father.

We were aware that this would not be an easy job. Since there was no hot water available, we could not scrape the pigs clean but had to skin them instead. Several neighbors came to watch this curiosity, wondering whether a missionary from the east and his assistant could perform such a difficult rural task.

I brought along my rifle to assist me. One of the men tried to convince me that it was impossible to kill a pig with a rifle shot. Now, I had not been raised on the reservation, but I was no city slicker either. I said to him, "We used to do it on the farm where I grew up as a child, and if it worked fine at that time, it'll work in Shiprock too." I then aimed two well-placed shots straight into the swine, and in each case the animal collapsed dead.

Soon both pigs were hanging in a large tree ready to be skinned. This part really was harder than we had anticipated. It was so hard to hold on to the greasy skin that we had to use pliers and our fingers cramped up and became stiff. But after a few hours the job was done. We left all the leftovers with a large pack of dogs that had obviously smelled the meat and were all too eager to clean up after us.

I returned home that evening with two butchered pigs in the back of my station wagon. Helen and the boys helped me to carry them into the basement of the parsonage where we cut them up the following day. I was having the time of my life as I made pork sausage, liver sausage, and even headcheese, all skills taken from my childhood. Our deep freezer was almost filled to the brim with meat. Neighbors were happy to have some of the fat and slabs of bacon which they enjoyed eating with boiled beans. We were well stocked with meat enough to last us more than a year.

More often we would butcher one of the birds I raised. One year, I had raised a large tom turkey that weighed in at 40 pounds. Preparing for butchering it, the boys and I tied it up and put it inside a gunnysack with only its head sticking out. Our son, David, sat on top of the bird to hold it down while I chopped off the bird's head with an ax. The headless bird, running on pure adrenaline, knocked David off its back and somehow managed to work itself loose and free. It flopped around in our back yard for quite a while. It was plucked and cleaned and cut up for the freezer. We also purchased two large bags of mountain-grown potatoes from one of the members of the church and a load of apples raised by another. Add to that a large bag of flour plus a few other basic items from the grocery store, there certainly couldn't be any worries about being snowed in that year.

It was a rather unique experience for our sons to grow up as they did among the Navajo as a missionary's kids. The following section was written by our son David describing some of that experience from his perspective:

Living on the Navajo reservation was really the only life I had ever known as a kid. If nothing else, it gave me an appreciation for other cultures. I was especially comfortable being with Navajos. In fact, after I had grown up and moved away from home, my best friends in Albuquerque were Navajos, including my best friend in college and the woman I would eventually marry, both of whom I met at the University of New Mexico. But even as a boy in Toadlena, there were several Navajo boys at church and at Newcomb School that I became good friends with.

I also learned to appreciate living in rural areas. Not only was Toadlena a very small community of perhaps 100 people, but it was so far from everything. We did shopping and errands in Farmington, 75 miles away. Therefore, Mom and Dad only shopped once every two weeks. When I was old enough, I often chose to stay home in Toadlena, and probably more than a few times spent over a month at a time without ever leaving the Toadlena/Newcomb area.

The word that comes to mind with this is contentment, at least as far as material possessions are concerned. I don't remember complaining about

Chapter Three: Toadlena

being so far from a pizza place, a K-Mart, a bowling alley, or a movie theatre. The thing my brothers and I sometimes laughed about was when we saw a TV commercial for a movie that was "coming soon to a theatre near you" when the nearest movie theatre was 75 miles away. I was content with living in Toadlena, and in fact enjoyed it.

But even if we were closer to town, we probably would not have seen many movies. Mom and Dad were very careful with what movies we saw. TV was the same way. Only a select few TV shows were permitted. Most game shows were OK; Little House on the Prairie was OK, as were The Brady Bunch and Gilligan's Island. Sports were also OK to watch, and as a result my brothers and I became avid sports fans--and we still are today. Star Trek was one of many forbidden shows. One evening, however, when Mom and Dad were gone, our baby sitters were watching Star Trek. I was already in bed, and wondered why Jack got to stay up so late. He finally came to bed and said he was supposed to be in bed, but he was watching Star Trek from the bottom of the stairs, and the babysitters never noticed him.

As far as going to church in Toadlena, there are some things that clearly stand out. One is that when we first moved there, some people would come to church on horseback or by horse and wagon. I was quite impressed with the patience these people had, as going to church and then back home probably took several hours. Another thing was the singing in the Navajo language, but it was something I got used to rather quickly, even though I didn't understand it. On the other hand, I found it very hard sitting through some long prayers and testimonies in Navajo.

I remember that, in church, every once in a while, some elderly ladies would hand me their Navajo songbook without saying a word. Mom had to explain to me that they simply wanted me to find the page for them, which I did. They never sang, and I doubt they could even read the songbook, but nevertheless they wanted to be part of the service in whatever way they could. True worship, of course, has nothing to do with being able to sing out of the book. Looking back, I'm glad that I could help them in that very small way.

Also, church in Toadlena was very informal, and I especially realized this when we were in church on vacation. The only good things about visiting churches back east were that services were conducted in English only and were much shorter than those in Toadlena. Other than that, I

Chapter Three: Toadlena

was terribly uncomfortable with formal clothing and not being allowed to look around or talk. Was I ever glad to get back to the Toadlena church where I could be myself! I didn't have to worry about wearing a coat or tie or sitting perfectly still. In Toadlena, it was perfectly acceptable to look around to see who was sitting behind me.

Dad raised lots of birds in Toadlena, mostly chickens and pigeons. When I was old enough, it was my job to help feed them, give them water, let them out in the morning, and put them in at night. Especially when Dad wasn't around, I was in charge and I was proud that I could do it by myself. Over the years the birds came to include turkeys, ducks and geese. Dad had built a small pond for the ducks and geese as well.

The geese were very good at keeping the neighbors' dogs away from the chickens, but that was the extent of the geese helping them out. We had a mean rooster who loved to attack children and even the ducks. But the rooster, as mean as he was, knew full well not to mess with the male goose. I learned to throw an empty Prestone container at the rooster when he felt like attacking me, which would work for a few days. Dad would take it a step further and regularly throw the rooster into the duck pond. That usually worked for about a week. Finally, one night the rooster met his match when I accidentally locked the geese inside the chicken coop. The next morning Dad saw the rooster lying on the ground, barely moving. Initially, I felt bad for the rooster, but then realized he deserved every bit of punishment he got!

One of the highlights of the year for my brothers and me was our annual Christmas shopping trip to Albuquerque. Every year, usually on the first Thursday in December, we would get three nights in the big city of Albuquerque, in a motel, which also meant three nights of color TV! Back home all we ever had was black and white. The color TV, shopping at Winrock Center, and getting a day off school made this annual event something to look forward to months in advance. For the first several years of our Albuquerque trip, we would stay at a small motel on Central Avenue--no doubt an old Route 66 place-- in a fairly rough part of town. That was the least of our concerns, as it was a two-room suite and of course, that meant not just one, but two color TV's—one in each room. Imagine the next morning getting to see Captain Kangaroo with a clear picture in color; this was living in luxury!

The next day was for shopping, and shopping meant Winrock Center.

Chapter Three: Toadlena

Winrock Center had escalators at Montgomery Ward, among other stores and attractions, but by far our favorite place there was Ben Franklin. Ben Franklin had all the gifts we would need to find for the whole family, including plenty of toys and football cards. Another thing Ben Franklin had was a cafeteria where Jack and I, when old enough, would pair up with either Jim or Mark for lunch—separate from Mom and Dad. We were proud of the fact that we could do lunch on our own.

From time to time over the years, Mom suggested to Dad that we go to the rival mall, Coronado Center, only about a mile away from Winrock. Dad did not want to mess with more than one shopping center while in Albuquerque, though one year we tried Coronado for Mom's sake. We boys hated it. Among other things, it didn't seem to have any toys, and certainly no Ben Franklin, so Mom didn't have a chance in those days. All four of us boys supported Dad. After we moved to Tohatchi in 1981, not only, had we gotten older, and with that our excitement had faded; but also, they had just opened a K-Mart in Gallup-only 24 miles from home. The good old days of Christmas shopping in Albuquerque were gone.

Living in Toadlena offered little to no employment for just about anybody. Jack and I, when we were old enough, were no exception to this, especially being Anglo. But Mom and Dad did not let that stop them from teaching us good work ethics. From a very young age, we most certainly helped with household chores (dishes, garbage, helping Dad care for the chickens and pigeons, etc.). Every now and then, Dad, my brothers and I would drive along the roads, collecting empty pop bottles—back in the days when soda pop came in glass bottles. After collecting enough of them and cleaning them out, we would bring them to the store for a nickel per bottle. We would also sit outside Newcomb Trading Post once or twice a year selling some of Dad's pigeons, for which my brothers and I got all the profit.

One of my cousins, when he and I were both teenagers, while visiting us in Toadlena with his family, asked me point blank, "How can you live in a place like this with nothing to do?" My answer was that, if it's where you grow up and its the only life you know, you get used to it. Looking back, not only is it something my brothers and I got used to, but something I believe we all came to appreciate. Without question, spending our childhood years on the reservation has made our lives richer and more

81

Chapter Three: Toadlena

complete. And we also had plenty to do as far as recreation goes, though admittedly at times we had to be very creative.

Being a missionary's kid has given me an appreciation for missions. Praying for missionaries, supporting them financially or perhaps becoming a missionary someday—either short-term or full-time—is something all Christians should be doing regularly. The last thing Jesus said, in Matthew 28:19, before He went back into heaven was for us to "Go and make disciples of all nations." I am certainly thankful for the years I spent on the mission field and my life is definitely richer because of it.

-- David Klumpenhower

A RAW ENVIRONMENT

Located in a mostly empty desert, Toadlena and the area around it could receive some interesting weather. The winters could be surprisingly cold, and where we were up against the mountain, we got a fair amount of snow to go with it. Spring was often hot and dry, followed by a rainier late summer and fall.

Those hot, windy spring days could be particularly memorable. One April day, a few days before income taxes were due, we realized that, for some reason, we had almost forgotten to pay our dues to Uncle Sam. I had even neglected to get the necessary tax forms, and the only place to get them was at the bank in Shiprock. There was no choice but to go there and drive the ninety miles there and back it would take to get them.

As I left the house and looked over the valley, I noticed that in some areas the dust was blowing high into the air. This was quite normal during the spring when strong winds would come to the area. The longer I drove on, the stronger the winds became and the dust clouds were getting thicker. Thousands of tumbleweeds skittered across the highway at high speed. About halfway to Shiprock, the dust became so bad that it was impossible to see. I had been following a large truck but even lost sight of it in the terrible mass of sand flying through the air. There was no other option but to park along the highway and to wait for the dust storm to clear. The wind was howling and the sand was coming inside the car and became caked on the inside of the windows. I tied a handkerchief around my nose in order to breathe. Everything around me was getting even darker. I have to admit that it was a scary situation. I was certainly glad that Helen and the children were not with me.

After some time the wind calmed down enough for me to see a ways and I decided to move ahead carefully. As I pulled back onto the road, I suddenly found myself headed straight for the ditch on the opposite side of the road as the wind continued to pummel the vehicle from the right. This obviously indicated that I had better wait a bit longer and just let the car get sandblasted a little more. Finally the wind let up and I was able to drive on, albeit very cautiously. I did manage to make it to Shiprock and return home that day, but I learned to avoid dust storms in the future. With all the sand that got into the carburetor and engine, our car never ran well again.

These dust storms sometimes even managed to make their way all the way into the foothills where we lived. In those circumstances, we simply had to close all the windows in the house and wait it out.

Then again, come the late summer months, one could also get caught in terrible rainstorms when the monsoon rains arrived. Flash floods rushing down through the mountain valleys turned quiet arroyo beds into sudden raging rivers. These rains could also make for driving problems. The rain could come down so hard that it did almost no good to the dry land as the water simply washed away. Driving on a wet dirt road could become almost impossible as much of the soil turned into a sticky clay on the surface. Keeping control of your vehicle was nearly impossible. Trying to walk in that clay was even worse as boots could quickly accumulate several inches of the ooze as it sank deep into the ground.

One day, I was surprised by a sudden monsoon while driving down a mountain dirt road. A young couple from the church was with me to help me find the way to someone's house up the mountain. It was too dangerous to continue driving on the wet trail, for we could very easily slide into the deep ravines next to us. We waited patiently for the sun to come out and to dry the trail but to no avail. The couple with me finally took the shovel I always carried in the back of the truck and scraped a dry trail ahead of me for at least a mile. Slowly but surely we reached home again that day.

Chapter Three: Toadlena

Our family enjoyed living on the mountainside. It was a treat to sit out in the yard in the evening when things could be so quiet that you could hear nothing except for an odd fly or buzzing bee. The temperature would drop immediately once the sun went down behind the mountain ridge to our west and we usually needed to put on a jacket or sweater to keep from getting cold. At an altitude of 7000 feet above sea level, things cooled off quickly after sunset. Toadlena was an easy place to stargaze. In those clear skies far away from cities of any size, we often watched shooting stars zip by and occasionally were privileged to see comets. These were sights many other people in the country did not have the privilege to view.

We had a homemade grill where we could build a fire and have some coffee or cook some hamburgers. One of our neighboring families would sometimes come over to join us by the grill. We had fun as we swapped stories of earlier times and shared laughs together. They shared how they as children used to play church just as we used to do. When I would play church as a child with my friends and family, we always put more importance on who would collect the offering and who would do the preaching, but these things had not been very important to this Navajo family. What was important to them was the time of handshaking with each other. They would go around and shake hands with the tree branches pretending that the trees were people.

Our children also enjoyed their quiet surroundings. It was a wide open land where one could let his creativity run on endlessly, and the boys were quite active within the spaciousness of the place. Instead of having more traditional pets, not counting the stray cats or dogs that frequented the grounds, we gave them some pet lambs. I also managed to raise some chickens, geese, turkeys, ducks, and pigeons. There was plenty of room for a vegetable garden, and, blessed with the church's own plentiful supply of water from its well, we were able to grow all the vegetables our family needed.

Practically the whole reservation was open range land where cattle and other livestock could wander all over. When people put up a fence, as the church had around its property, it was done not so much to keep their animals inside, but rather to keep them out. This, too, could take some getting used to, such as the time on one otherwise quiet night when we were rudely awakened by a sudden loud noise just outside of our bedroom window. It sounded as if someone was screaming at us in some unintelligible language. I jumped out of bed, only to see that it was the neighbor's donkey which had somehow managed to get past the fence barrier. As long as we lived in New Mexico, it was not uncommon for myself or one of the boys to have to go out to chase a horse or cow off the property when one had wandered in after someone left a stray gate open.

CHANGING TIMES

The Christian Church was often criticized by outsiders for being culturally insensitive on the reservation. The major critics were those who adhered to the traditional Navajo religion and the white people who were employed on the reservation. Some of the criticism was valid as the church is not without fault, but not all of it was deserved. Many churches encouraged the people to keep the good things of their culture while putting away that which is not good as all people must do when they embrace the Christian faith. We encouraged the people to keep their language and to use it as we offered Navajo reading classes to them. Some traditional practices could be changed into Christian practices by making a few alterations. This was the case in house dedication ceremonies or the ceremony at the time of a baby's first laugh. On several occasions I was asked to lead in a house dedication by a Christian family. This turned into a wonderful event where a group of believers gathered in the house and spent time together to sing praises to the Lord and to pray for God's blessing on the home and the family. People brought food to such a meeting and celebrated with the family. On Sundays, we occasionally had a ceremony for a baby's first laugh. It was a time of feasting and of singing hymns of praise together followed by parents dedicating the child to the Lord. There was no need to lose some of these fine cultural values in that they in no way conflicted with the Gospel.

Regardless, the culture was being changed anyway. Over the years we noticed that many advancements were coming to the reservation. More people were now blessed with electricity in their homes and running water. The Navajo government worked at helping the older generation and families with many children obtain better housing, even though a few of the older people did not appreciate this help. One older couple had lived in a small and old house all their life and, when a new house was built for them, they refused to occupy it. When I asked them why they did not move into the new house equipped with electricity and running water, they answered, "We don't feel at home in there."

The coming of modern utilities such as these brought big changes to the people. Electric appliances came onto the scene and, of course, the television. The people had a big appetite for movies and Hollywood brought many changes that were not always so good. A cultural gap developed between the younger and older generation and many of the older people became deeply concerned as they could not keep pace with the younger ones. It was sad to see so many people become addicted to an ungodly and worldly lifestyle, replacing solid traditional values with unwholesome and godless teachings of modern life.

More public schools were now being built where children could be bussed to school and back home in the evening. This had advantages over the government boarding schools where children were deprived of their family life. In our opinion, in most cases, it is a big advantage for a child to be able to live at home. Although the Boarding Schools gave the children a decent education and even offered the community some opportunities for employment, they, like all boarding schools, helped to raise a generation of youth who did not know how to be part of a family.

DIFFICULTIES FROM WITHIN

An indigenous church is a church that is self-governing, self-propagating, and financially self-supporting. These are goals that a healthy emerging church should strive to achieve. Most of our small churches on the reservation were far from being indigenous even though they had been in existence for several decades. With the help and encouragement from the Mission Board, we were challenged to address this situation and hopefully remove any obstacles that stood in the way of achieving this goal.

The matter of churches becoming self-governing could only be solved through giving more instruction in the churches to its members. In order to do so, all missionary personnel were in need of multiple training sessions after which they would share their learning with their respective churches. Lectures were given on effective leadership and in training elders and deacons and Sunday school teachers for more effective service. Training was given in church government and polity. We looked at different options of church leadership such as full-time pastors, part-time pastors, and pastors who would work on a voluntary basis while holding a regular job to provide for their financial income.

Our churches had been self-propagating, but over the years the rate of church growth was low compared to many other places in the world. This has alarmed many people and in particular it caused Mission Boards and supporters of Native American mission activity some concern. At times, blame was directed at mission personnel on the field both in the past and present. They were seen as ineffective and as being closed to new and better ways of ministry. Some of the criticism was warranted, but not all. Much was not constructive. It often reminded me of an old saying that the best captains of the ship are those who are standing on dry land.

Whatever the underlying reasons may be, it is my personal feeling that if any blame for slow propagation is warranted, most of it should not be directed to the Navajo Christians. The Christian Navajos have not been hesitant about reaching out to unbelievers with the gospel and their testimonies. They supported Navajo gospel programs that were broadcast all across the reservation. They organized and planned camp meetings at their churches where the gospel was preached to their unbelieving relatives and neighbors. We have always admired their faithful witnessing to relatives, friends, and coworkers, as well as their fervent prayers for the salvation of the lost. It is important that we take regular inventory of our ways of witnessing to the world, but at the same time we must accept the fact that not all fruit ripens quickly.

The matter of becoming financially self-supporting was certainly something desirable. It was seen as an eventual possibility for the larger churches and for those with a stronger financial base. For the smaller churches deeper on the reservation this was regarded as being out of reach for them unless they would accept a different leadership such as volunteer lay leaders who would carry out the work of ministry. The wisdom of such a change was questionable and was not working out well for many small church groups of other denominations who were practicing this. There came to be a fear among the Navajo churches that the CRC was going to abandon their small churches as the denomination appeared to renege on the promises to support. Possibly some of this thinking stemmed back even further to years when the federal government reneged on some treaties made with the Native American people.

From all the teaching and learning in our churches came some positive and gratifying results. There was a maturing in the churches with a greater feeling for the church program and more ownership of it, but our desired goals would not be achieved without difficulty. This was a very demanding period of time that placed big demands upon our missionary personnel.

Although there was the general agreement that changes needed to take place in our churches, the necessary changes were sometimes pushed too fast upon the people before they were prepared for them. This created unnecessary tension and resentment in some churches. The matter of having a church government that consisted of a minister and elders and deacons with a hierarchy consisting of Classes and a Synod was still foreign to many of the people. In my own church at Toadlena, the leaders kept demanding why the church should be part of a classis and a synod. One of our leaders once commented, "If we run into a problem that we cannot handle with the help of the Lord, we will ask our closest neighboring church for its advice. Why do we have to make everything so complicated"? Later, when a Navajo classis was formed, it was questionable whether the majority of our Navajo Christians had actually even spoken in favor of it.

We also struggled with getting more native men interested in the formal work of ministry in their own churches. The Rehoboth Christian School, which was formerly our Mission School, was doing a wonderful job of giving a Christian education and was highly respected in the area, but not many of its Navajo graduates were attracted to a career in the ministry. Their superior education equipped them for well-paying jobs with the Navajo government or the Federal government. The church was unable to compete with those wages and most promising youth were unwilling to make the required sacrifices that came with entering the ministry.

Another difficulty that had to be faced was the fact that some of our missionary personnel had worked for many years in the same location without opportunity for a new challenge somewhere else. Not only were the missionaries in need of a new challenge, but also the churches they had served faithfully needed a change. An attempt was made to shuffle all missionaries on the reservation, but that soon failed and had to be discontinued. The concept of moving missionaries somewhere else was not always understood either. One of the members of my church was deeply disturbed when he heard that our family might be asked to move. He said to me, "I hear that they want to take you away from us. If that is true, I'll take the matter to the local chapter house and we will fight to keep you here." I made an attempt to explain the situation, the reasons behind it all, and that the local chapter house really had no authority in this case, but what I said seemed to fall on deaf ears.

We also had to struggle through some new policies made in Michigan by the CRC that showed insensitivity to the people we ministered to which lacked their input. We were informed that after a certain date all churches were to accept the responsibility for paying for the utility costs of their pastors. While in some churches this may have been possible, for some of the poorest churches like ours this created an impossible situation. Our large and roomy parsonage was expensive to heat. The cost for propane gas during the winter months came to a whopping $1000 per month, even when many of the rooms were closed off to conserve heat. Such an expense was too much for our congregation to cover. It was also a very insensitive policy to lay on people who had to heat their small houses with a wood stove and then be told to pay for an expensive heating system in the home of the missionary. I was thankful when, upon my request, an exception was made for our church, but the Board did insist on implementing their policy after we left Toadlena later on, creating additional resentment, just as we had feared.

It was also difficult to teach the congregation the responsibility of the local church to take care of the maintenance of all the church buildings. It was understood that everyone had to pitch in when there was maintenance work to be done on the church building itself, but not on the parsonage. It was quite a natural opinion to have, since if all people had to naturally take care of the maintenance of their own home, likewise why wouldn't it be the missionary's responsibility to do the same for the house he lived in? We therefore took time that we could have used for ministry to do a lot of maintenance work. This seemed to meet with better approval.

It has always been comforting to us that the church belongs to Jesus. As we work for Him, we always experience a certain amount of pain and frustration and other difficulties, but there are also many blessings. We have the Lord's promise that, in spite of the difficulties we must face, He will keep His church and build it until the very end of time. Our share of difficulties within the church needed to be seen as challenges that could be overcome.

And these things could be the least of our difficulties.

A ROARING LION

During the summer months, people gathered together for different religious festivals such as squaw dances or fire dances. These would be held for a whole week, primarily in the evenings and late into the night. A little further up the mountainside, behind the parsonage, there was a place where they held fire dances. In the evening, they would build a large fire, and we could watch them dancing around it and hear them chanting to the beat of their drums. The sound was enough to give us the chills. The Christians at church told us of some of the godless things that were going on at those festivals and that they no longer wanted to participate in them as they used to do before their conversion.

At those festivals, certain people were cursed, including Christian missionaries who came to bring the gospel. These people also told us that the medicine men claimed that their curses were ineffective on Christian missionaries. This is testimony of the power of Jesus to protect His people—power greater than that of all evil

Chapter Three: Toadlena

powers. Evil power is no superstition, but, rather, real power with real ability to wreak havoc. These dances were a reminder to us that we needed to pray constantly for the Lord's protection from these evil powers. Thank God that those who live in the shadow of the almighty do not have to live in fear of evil.

We knew that the forces of evil wanted to put fear into us to intimidate us out of our work on the reservation, and the Devil is not above using those who are in his grip to do so. Once, when I was gone to attend a meeting somewhere, the telephone rang. A neighbor who had been drinking heavily called and tried to talk with Helen to let out his anger. In the course of their conversation, he said, "I'm going to come over and kill you and Mr. K. both." Helen hung up the phone. She was very careful before opening the door for people who came to the house that day and was relieved when I returned home that evening.

On another occasion, the telephone rang in the middle of the night and I got up to answer it. A deep, growling voice on the other end said, "I'm going to kill you." I asked for his name, but could not understand his mumbling. Then he repeated his message to me. I hung up on him and left the phone off the hook for the rest of the night so that we could not be bothered. We prayed for God's protection and went back to an uneventful sleep. Our confidence in God's protection was enough for us to get by on. Nothing further ever came from these two events.

One of the church members had developed some strange problems that puzzled us. She was very restless and unable to sleep at night. Afraid to be at home during the night, she would walk all over the neighborhood. We became concerned about her health as she was looking pale and very tired.

We suggested that she sleep in our house for a night and hopefully catch some much needed rest. She accepted our offer and came over. During our evening prayer she got up from the table and went to her bedroom. We thought that this was rather strange for her and that she was not acting her normal self. During the night when we were all asleep, she got up and set the kitchen table using paper plates that she found in the cupboard and then she placed a marble on each plate. It became clear that she needed help, but we

Chapter Three: Toadlena

were at a loss on how to help her. It had also become clear to us that she became restless whenever we mentioned the name "Jesus" to her.

Arrangements were made by her family for her to meet with a psychiatrist in Shiprock. After several sessions with him, the problem remained as bad as ever. Eventually the psychiatrist came to Toadlena and asked to talk with me. I told him that my suspicion was demonic activity because of her reaction when she heard the name "Jesus".

He suggested that I read a Bible verse to her that spoke of Jesus. Although she only understood Navajo, I did not have my Navajo Bible with me, so I decided to read to her out of the English Bible. I read from Matthew 28:18 where Jesus says, "All authority in heaven and on earth has been given to me—", but after I read the first two words she immediately went into very heavy breathing and got up off her chair and ran out of the house. The psychiatrist was not prepared for such a reaction and blamed me for reading the wrong passage from the Bible, since I should have read something more "soothing" to her, perhaps regardless of the translation. He must have concluded that my wrong choice of scripture was the cause of her deep depression.

A few days after this, our family left to attend a Missionary Internship meeting in Farmington, Michigan, just east of Detroit. This was a three-week event sponsored by our Mission Board. We heard some excellent lectures on mission work. One of our instructors who had served for years as a missionary in Africa mentioned that the church in Africa was battling a lot of demonic activity. It was mentioned that Christians there sometimes suffered from what she called Demonic Depression. These people become very restless and often went into heavy breathing and would run away when they heard about the power and authority of Jesus. This confirmed my worst fears that the lady in my church was suffering from demonic activity and that, even though she herself had not been able to understand my reading from the English Bible, the demons did understand. There was a sense of fear in my knowing that now I would have to be willing to deal with the problem and confront it after getting back home.

When we returned home, I was relieved to hear that the

problem had disappeared. One of the Navajo Christians had taken the lady to a pastor with Pentecostal leanings who recognized the problem immediately and proceeded to cast three demons out of her in the name of Jesus. This pastor had learned things that I had never been taught in my training and he had the courage to face the demon world. Through this experience I gained some important orientation into working as a missionary on the front line of battle where Satan and his demons put up a struggle to keep a hold on people. These demonic forces were no match against the authority and power of Jesus. The lady's problem was gone and did not return.

The principal and vice-principal of the Toadlena Boarding School asked if they could come to visit as they were looking for advice with some problems at the school. They were concerned about the girls in the school who at certain times seemed to go berserk and would roll on the floor and foam at the mouth. These girls were out of control at such times and were filled with fear. The girls said that this occurred when they played "Holy Spirit", something they had copied from some of the more fanatically charismatic Christian groups on the reservation. Also, it was mentioned that in the school, the staff had seen some paranormal activity, such as tables moving and hanging lamps swaying without cause. The school staff wanted to know if there really was truth to demonic activity and if something could be done to stop it.

Our Bible Woman, who, although still a new Christian, was familiar with the demonic world and volunteered to meet with the schoolgirls. The school staff gladly cooperated with her and had her meet with all the girls in one of the rooms. The girls were told that what was happening to them was not something caused by Jesus for Jesus does not bring people fear, but contentment and joy.

Suddenly one of the girls fell off her chair and began to roll on the floor with foam coming out of her mouth. Our Bible Woman put her arm around the girl and said, "Satan, in the name of Jesus come out of this girl." Immediately the girl snapped out of it and was completely normal. The school had no more problems after that. The principal asked us, "What did you do to help us?" We were able to share with him and the rest of the school staff the wonderful power of Jesus over the evil forces in the world.

Chapter Three: Toadlena

Members of the church frequently shared some of their experiences with demonic forces. One told us how that the night after he had committed his life to Jesus he felt that someone was trying to choke him. He called out for help to Jesus, "Jesus, help me." The choking stopped and his life was spared. Other members have told us that they heard strange noises and saw strange beings. This was the case with a busload of students from Newcomb Junior High School. On the way home from a basketball game in Shiprock, they passed a rocky peak. It was said that when demons passed through this particular area, the rock was one of their resting places. When the bus rode past the rock that evening, the students began to scream and were completely out of control as they all saw demons coming into the bus. Somehow, the driver managed to drive the bus safely back to Newcomb School that evening. A pastor in that area prayed with the students and they all calmed down. Another time, Helen and I made a visit with a young lady in the hospital who was disturbed after having seen demons on the wall in her hospital room. They were making fun of her and laughing at her for having committed her life to Jesus. The demons said to her repeatedly, "We're going to get you back. We're going to get you back." We spent time in prayer with her. Tragically, not long thereafter she became involved in a sin that caused her to leave the church. To this day she has not returned and has turned against the Christian way.

Then it happened to me one Sunday when I was praying in church shortly before the worship service was to begin that suddenly I became depressed. Someone seemed to be telling me, "Don't you preach what you have planned to preach." My plan was to preach on I Peter 5:8-9 where the Lord warns us against Satan, the roaring lion, looking for someone to devour. I felt that this depression was from Satan, attempting to intimidate me. With trust in the Lord for his help and protection, I was able to tell the enemy that I would certainly preach as I had planned and with all the power the Lord would give me. This experience shook me up, however, and when I led the worship service at Newcomb that same afternoon, I was still shaking some and began to cry and told the worshipers what had happened to me that morning. They understood me well. One by one they stood up and either spoke a word of encouragement or read a verse from scripture and prayed for me. It turned into a powerful service of praise to God.

TOWARDS THE END OF OUR TOADLENA TENURE

The mission at Toadlena was growing, but the growth was admittedly slow. The church numbered about 80 worshipers on Sunday mornings. This was a pretty good group considering that we were in a sparsely populated area in the heart of the reservation. After all the years of hard work, we had seemingly barely made a dent. Besides the Enemy that was constantly opposing our efforts, there were other factors to be reckoned with. Due to the lack of employment, the younger and more aggressive people moved away to greener pastures to work and live. Those left behind were mostly more traditional older people and people who had become apathetic in life. The problems brought on by alcoholism were severe and affected almost every family in one way or another. It caused a lot of abuse, marriage problems, dishonesty, distrust, etc. Naturally, people brought these problems with them into the church and the church had to learn to deal with them. Only Jesus could build a thriving church in such a community.

One of my neighbors was coming to the parsonage again to use the telephone. This in itself was fine, as he did so frequently, except for that this time he was heavily under the influence of alcohol. I told him that, since he had been drinking and was not in shape to use the telephone, he therefore would have to come back another day. He became very angry and scolded me.

When I went back into my office to finish reading my daily devotions, I read in 2 Thessalonians 3:15 where it says, "Do not regard him as an enemy, but warn him as a brother." This verse spoke directly to me and made me feel guilty for what I had done. Instead of just dismissing his need and sending him home, I should at least have asked whether he had an emergency or even whether I could make the call for him. I went to his house to apologize, but he was not at home. Instead, however, the following morning, he came to apologize to me for having been so angry and for scolding me. He admitted that I had done the right thing to send him home

Chapter Three: Toadlena

and admitted that he had been drinking.

Nonetheless, this episode was evidence of the wearisome nature of the job we had and the toll it was taking. After working for eight years at Toadlena, Helen and I were beginning to tire some. We asked ourselves if it might be better for us and the church if we moved to work somewhere else. Even a few relational problems began to show up between us and some of the leading people of the church. We decided that we should pray that the Lord would give us some sort of confirmation if He wanted us to stay at Toadlena.

We received the Lord's confirmation the very next day. Floyd and I were out doing campwork, and as we were approaching a house, the man who lived there was standing by the house waiting for us as if he was expecting our arrival. This seemed strange to us, especially seeing as how prior to this he had never shown much interest in our visits. He came to our vehicle and said to us, "Please come inside. I have something to tell you." We obliged and he told his story.

"As I was sleeping last night, I had a terrible nightmare," he said. "I dreamt I was working outside by the house when suddenly I noticed many demons coming towards me from all sides. They wanted to kill me, and, because I was encircled, there was no escape for me. I was terribly afraid, but," he continued, "then I heard a noise and saw you missionaries coming in your vehicle. When the demons saw you coming, they all fled and left me alone."

Immediately I recognized that this was the confirmation that Helen and I had prayed for. The Lord was telling me that there was still work to be done by us and that we could still bring people what they needed. We could do our work without fear, for we had a power on our side that was far superior to all evil powers combined. Helen and I were encouraged through this and the Lord continued to bless us with another four years of work at Toadlena after that.

Three years later, in August of 1980, towards the end of our tenure at Toadlena, we were offered a six-month sabbatical to study more of the Navajo language and culture. We would be living in Flagstaff, Arizona and become full-time students. Two other missionary couples—The Brummels and Stuits—would be joining us. This was a wonderful offer to us from our Mission Board and we accepted it. This kind of study was likely to have benefits for us in the years ahead.

Arrangements were made for Floyd to take care of things at the Toadlena church during this time and we moved as a family to Flagstaff. We knew that this would be a big change for us and for our children as well. We would be once again living off of the reservation and the boys would be attending schools which were predominantly populated by White children. None of the children, particularly the youngest two, had had much regular everyday exposure to their own "white" culture.

The study itself was helpful to us, but those six months were perhaps the most difficult ones of our lives, at least intellectually. We were bombarded daily with the Navajo language and worked at it day and night until we could practically feel it in our bones. We were expected to talk with Navajos in their native language conversationally.

Navajo is one of the most difficult languages in the world and it is said that it takes an average of thirty years to master it. This was part of the reason why it could be used so effectively as a code in World War II against Japan. The Navajo people are quite proud of this contribution, and rightly so, as the code talkers contributed much to the final victory in the war. The Japanese, in all the effort they put into it, were never able to crack the code. How were we supposed to learn it then?

Of equal benefit to us was the training in Navajo culture and religion. This did prove quite helpful in our later years on the reservation. In the meantime, our sons adjusted and gained valuable insight into life off the reservation.

FAREWELLS

In March of 1981, we returned to Toadlena. There we were notified that the church in Tohatchi, NM—a somewhat larger town about 50 miles to the south and about 25 miles north of Gallup—was looking for a new pastor. Another pastor and I were under their current consideration. This ultimately resulted in a call for me to minister there, which we accepted.

For several years prior we had felt an attraction to the work

Chapter Three: Toadlena

there whenever we passed through the area on our way to Gallup. On one of those trips, we even took time out to drive through the town and to see what all was there. It was a school town composed of two government boarding schools and a full range of public schools. It seemed like a challenge for any missionary couple who enjoyed working with school children beyond the normal work of the ministry. We had no idea that one day we would actually be asked to move there.

Tohatchi also appealed to us for our children's sake as they would be within walking distance to school and finally have easy opportunities to be involved in after-school activities. This had generally been impossible at Toadlena as they had to be bussed 12 miles to the elementary/junior high school in Newcomb, or a full 45 miles to the high school in Shiprock. This distance had not entirely kept Jack or David from being excluded from participating in extracurricular activities, but it made those possibilities problematic at best. Also, since Tohatchi was a mere 25 miles from the city of Gallup, a short distance for anyone used to living on the wide open reservation, there was far more opportunity for summer jobs for the boys, and this too was important to us.

For the following thirteen years, then, Tohatchi would be our home. We moved there in August of 1981 to begin a new challenge which we took on with great anticipation, believing that the Lord would be there as well to help us. Our sons, however, were quite attached to Toadlena, and did not share the enthusiasm for the move we had. For the youngest ones, Toadlena was the only home they ever knew. They had grown to appreciate not only their friends there, but also that old, large house which they had grown up in and the wide open mountain spaces that surrounded them. It was a difficult move for them, as one might expect. They would always consider Toadlena their "home".

The Toadlena church and community gave us a big farewell and showered us with many gifts and good wishes. Many shared their appreciation for the years we had spent with them. Everyone seemed pleased that, although we were moving away, we would remain on the reservation and within reach. The church is still there today in Toadlena, but as a smaller congregation. It is led by one of the lay members who serves as their pastor and preacher.

The old parsonage where we lived, however, is no longer there as it burned completely to the ground in 1999. Due to being in such a remote location, the fire truck had to come all the way from Shiprock. By the time firefighters arrived, all that was left were smoldering ashes.

Some weeks after the fire, Helen and I went to see the site of the old house. It is always tragic when something that holds as many vivid memories as that is lost forever, and it now felt as if an important part of our lives had been taken away from us. Here, deep in the heart of the reservation, we had been through many other sorts of fires in this same place, but never with this utter feeling of loss evidenced in the charred heaps laying at our feet. This, then, looked to be how the final chapter of our Toadlena story would play out.

Still, we wandered among the ashes. But as we looked among the rubble, we saw a portion of an old cardboard box that had survived unscathed through the fire, partially buried in the debris. We lifted it out to reveal the large letters long ago written on its side: "Helen Klumpenhower."

Something still there after 18 years and even enduring the fire. It was hard to describe the emotions flowing deep within us at that point, but somehow we knew that, through it all, we must have successfully left our mark there.

CHAPTER 4

Tohatchi

FIRST NAVAJO CHRISTIAN REFORMED CHURCH

Herman Fryling and Andrew VanderWagon were the first pioneer missionaries sent by our denomination to bring the gospel to the Navajo people. These men and their families arrived in Ft. Defiance, Arizona in 1896 and were the first to begin Bible instruction classes for the children at the government boarding school in Ft. Defiance.

The work at Ft. Defiance proved to be very difficult and discouraging, mostly due to opposition from the Roman Catholic Church. The Catholic priests had begun their mission activities a few decades earlier and understandably did not appreciate any competition from Protestants.

About 40 miles to the east, across the Chuska mountain range, was the community of Tohatchi, New Mexico. The community was known for a government boarding school that was headed by a Christian principal. The Roman Catholic Church was not active in that part of the reservation at that time. The missionaries at Ft. Defiance decided to investigate the possibility of beginning mission work in Tohatchi. VanderWagon took a trip in 1898 across the mountain by horse and wagon to obtain more information on the Tohatchi area and school. The school principal was delighted to meet with him and encouraged him to begin Bible instruction classes for the Tohatchi children. She also proposed that the school help to secure a mission site.

The following year a four-acre tract was secured from the federal government and construction was begun on an adobe house for a resident missionary and a barn to house his horse and milk cow. In the meantime, some Bible instruction classes were held at

Chapter Four: Tohatchi

the Tohatchi boarding school by VanderWagon and Fryling.

The first resident missionary was James DeGroot. It was pioneer work with few conveniences. Medical problems caused by high altitude forced DeGroot to stop his work and move away after one year. He was succeeded by a young missionary, L.P. Brink, who later served in Toadlena. With his new bride, he made his home in Tohatchi for the next thirteen years.

It was here that Brink worked at translating parts of the Bible into Navajo. He also produced a booklet of hymns in the Navajo language. In the meantime, a training school was begun for Navajo assistants to give them the necessary Bible information to carry the gospel message to their own people all across the reservation. Due to his wife's illness, Brink also was compelled to leave Tohatchi and was replaced by Lee Huizenga who was both a minister and a medical doctor. With the assistance of a Navajo interpreter, he spent much of his time traveling on horseback all across the countryside to visit the sick and at the same time to demonstrate the love of Jesus to the people and bring the gospel message. This medical missionary stayed for six years and left because he had dedicated himself to working as a missionary in China. He left in 1920. Later, he and his wife were murdered in China by communist soldiers who did not appreciate the Gospel.

After these first few people, the Tohatchi mission continued with a long list of faithful missionaries and assistants who have worked there over the years. Among them were Edward Becenti, J.C. Morgan, Mark Bouma, Ned Plummer, Walter Bitsie, William Goudberg, Ben DeBoer, Alfred Bowman, Clarence Chischilly, Guy Lee, Louis Henry, G. Pars, J.R. Kamps, Gordon Stuit, Edward Henry, Frank Curley, Albert Henry, Ernest Benally, Edgar Bitsoie, Thelma VanderVen, Ted Charles, Howard Begay, and Howard Redhouse. Our family followed this long list of faithful workers. I have always found it interesting that four of the first five missionaries were struggling with severe health problems that disrupted their service or forced them to have to leave. It appears that Satan was trying his best to prevent the spread of the gospel as he is still doing all across the world today.

In the early days, the water source for the mission was down

Chapter Four: Tohatchi

a steep hill about 1000 feet away where a small spring left a small pool of water. The water had to be scooped with a cup into a pail and then carried up the steep hill and to the house. I have been told by the older Navajo residents of Tohatchi that the name "Tohatchi" means "scratching for water" and derived its name from the little pool of spring water. Later, a well was drilled at that place and the well water was pumped into a tank in the barn and from there to the missionary house.

A beautiful church building was erected in 1910, a towering building which contrasted greatly with the rest of the area's structures. The parsonage was built in the late 1920s. Some years later, a house for an assistant was also constructed.

The church building is certainly an interesting feature of the Tohatchi mission. It prominently features several large, old stained glass picture windows, each perhaps ten-feet-tall, that were donated by a druggist in Holland, Michigan and imported from Italy. Amazingly, these have never been broken. One of the windows has a beautiful picture of Jesus the Good Shepherd carrying a sheep in his arms. A second window pictures Jesus knocking on the door. The third window pictures Jesus returning on the clouds of heaven. Many of the older Navajo people who used to attend school and come to the church building for Bible instruction still remember clearly the pictures in the windows and its messages, even though they never became Christians or attended worship services in the building. With its cathedral-like architecture, complete with a bell tower on the roof, the church building is undoubtedly the tallest building in the community and is easily spotted from nearly every vantage point in town. Today, this building is of historical value and still very much in use. It is a demonstration of the love for mission outreach to the Navajo people by those who built it and paid for it.

Over the years, the building has become a landmark for the whole community and still graces the countryside with its beauty. While I was in the church building one day, I heard some people coming inside. It was a middle-aged couple who looked like tourists. They were speaking to each other using Dutch, my mother tongue. They were greatly surprised when I said to them, "Ik kan ook wel Hollands spreken." They were astonished to find someone

103

Chapter Four: Tohatchi

way out here on the Navajo reservation speaking their language. Their reason for coming was to look over our beautiful church building which they had apparently seen from the highway. I gave them a brief history of myself and what brought me to Tohatchi and a brief history of the church. As they left, they handed me a small card with their identification. These were apparently upper-class people and the man was a high official in the Dutch government. A few days after they left, the same couple sent us a note of thanks and it included a $50 bill designated for use towards our mission at Tohatchi.

Still, the most beautiful part of the Tohatchi church, as with all of God's church, is the congregation that meets there faithfully. As the first congregation established on the reservation, they are officially known as "First Navajo Christian Reformed Church." These people have always understood that they are to be God's tools in continuing to bring the gospel of Jesus to their community as they have remained actively involved within it.

Besides the regular work of reaching out through the schools, the Tohatchi mission also served as the community post office for several years. This was an excellent help in keeping contact with the community.

Tohatchi lay at the base of the southern end of the Chuska mountains. Some 5 or 10 miles to the west of Tohatchi was Chuska Peak, where it was said that the demons lived. From that high peak, these spirits went out all over the land to do their work. The medicine man had great respect for Chuska Peak and worshipped his gods on that peak. I had heard that one of our former missionaries and his assistant had climbed the peak and prayed on that mountain and claimed it for Jesus in response to this belief.

THE WORK BEGINS

When we were called to serve there in 1981, Tohatchi was quite a bit larger than Toadlena. At this time, however, attendance at church had been low and workers were stretched thin. Rev. Edward Henry, with his wife, Ella, was serving as missionary pastor at Tohatchi Mission at this time. The assistant who had worked with Pastor Henry had resigned and the staff was in big need of help. We

Chapter Four: Tohatchi

made an agreement to serve in a team ministry with the Henrys for the next two years when he would reach the time of his retirement.

The Henrys suggested that they vacate the larger parsonage and move into the assistant house as our family was larger and needed more space. Also, this would eliminate the need for us to move again in two years, even if just across the driveway. We accepted this generous gesture. The congregation made a point of painting the inside of the parsonage before we moved in and even laid new carpet in the living room since the old carpet was badly worn.

The parsonage was no more than 50 feet from the church building. We knew that we would much appreciate the convenience of living so close to it with no steep hill to climb as in Toadlena. Our sons, with their long legs, used to claim that it took twelve (leaping) steps to go from the parsonage to the church entrance, but for Helen and me, it was a little farther than that.

The old barn with its attached chicken coop provided plenty of space for my chickens and other birds that I brought from Toadlena. These birds were helpful as they gave me the needed respite from the daily routine of work. I never did forget what my father told me one day when we were visiting with him on his farm in Ontario. He told me, "It seems easier for me to work with cows every day than with people." From his years of experience serving as deacon or elder in the church, he had become keenly aware that people can be difficult to work with. Although I have always enjoyed working with people and ministering to them on behalf of Jesus, I must agree that my father's observation was correct at least for much of the time.

My main task at Tohatchi was to serve as missionary/pastor of the church, although a large portion of my time was spent in the teaching of Bible Classes for school children. The Tohatchi congregation was quite small and consisted of mostly older people. The church had found itself in a rut and seemed to lack a sense of purpose and mission. Outreach to the younger generation had been neglected. Over the years there had been a

Chapter Four: Tohatchi

gradual decline in church attendance to about 40 worshipers on a Sunday morning.

The congregation had some positive elements, however. The worshipers were solid in the Christian faith and in attending meetings. The church was also blessed with having men, as well as women, in attendance, while in many churches or mission stations the women far outnumbered the men. This came out of a tradition where the women usually took on more responsibility for the family and the children while the men had the tendency to hold back. It was refreshing to see several good and faithful Christian men, husbands and fathers, in this church.

The attendance began to gradually increase. Some visitors came out of curiosity while others had a genuine interest in hearing the Word of God. One Sunday morning two ladies came to church for the first time. They simply explained to the congregation that they had come because "they were looking for Jesus."

Young people and young couples began to attend worship services also. They had heard that I preached in the English language and they appreciated that as they had limited understanding of their native language. They had a special interest in learning about the Christian home and Christian marriage. One year, I gave pre-marriage counseling to five separate couples. They enjoyed these lessons so much that in most cases the couples asked for additional lessons. After some basic lessons on the Christian faith, each of these couples committed their lives to the Lord. Four of the five couples joined the Tohatchi church. Over the years, other couples followed the initial five. Evidently there was a great need for this ministry and I enjoyed doing it. Through this, the congregation was fast becoming younger. Some of the men who received the instruction are serving as elders and deacons in the Tohatchi church today and their wives are taking an active part in church activities also.

One young couple was eager for a Christian wedding at the church, but the bride's parents were not cooperating. They were Roman Catholic and still had leanings toward the traditional Navajo religion. The parents threatened to disown their daughter as

Chapter Four: Tohatchi

Lillian and Kenneth Jones get married in Tohatchi Church.

a member of the family and to prevent the wedding. Eventually the couple was encouraged by members of the church to proceed with their planned wedding, even if her parents and some other family members might not be present. In lieu of other family members being there, the rest of the Tohatchi church agreed to be present for the wedding and to serve as family by bringing food and by joining in the celebration, essentially replacing the bride's family and its role.

It was a beautiful wedding, despite the obvious absence of her family. But, to our surprise, the father of the bride came to quietly observe from the back of the church. There was yet an even bigger surprise waiting for us. Just as the reception dinner was to begin, the parents came in weeping. Immediately the bride ran to greet her parents and hugged them and had them sit at the table reserved for the bridal party. Tears were wiped away and the celebration continued.

There were a lot of requests for catechism training and teaching in church membership. I have always felt that this can best be done in individual homes rather than in groups. Two of the church's leading families were willing to help with this work. After going through the lessons themselves, they went out to teach those who

Chapter Four: Tohatchi

Everett and Martha Manuelito teach catechism in a home.

requested it. The result of this was frequent baptisms and professions of faith. We were gathering in the harvest and our church building was now beginning to fill up on Sundays.

Ella Henry passed away in 1982 after a struggle with cancer. Her husband, Edward, reached retirement age the following year and left Tohatchi. This left us short of help, but around the reservation there were some young Navajo couples in training for the ministry. For some years we had one couple at a time work with us as pastor interns. We were then receiving extra help while they were getting on-the-job training in ministry. These interns helped with teaching classes and with some of the family visiting. They did some occasional preaching as well. In return, I instructed them in a Bible survey, making sermons, and church polity. This arrangement worked out quite well for us. It's rewarding to see that two of the interns that worked and trained with us are still serving as full-time pastors on the reservation today.

SCHOOL TOWN

Once we were settled somewhat with moving into the parsonage, it was time to give our attention to our oldest son, Jack.

Chapter Four: Tohatchi

He had graduated from Shiprock High School earlier that spring. Now his sights were set on attending the University of Missouri where he planned to major in journalism. Since we had just moved, it was not a favorable time for us to take time off so soon and bring him to his school in person, something we felt rather bad about. Instead, he left by bus from Gallup in a pouring rain during the middle of the night. To see our first son leave home, especially in this way, gave us some anxiety, but it was mixed with parental pride that he had reached this milestone in his life.

Tohatchi was a school town. There were two large government boarding schools and a public high school, middle school, and elementary school. We were permitted to give weekly Bible instruction after school hours at both of the boarding schools. At one of the two schools, they offered us the use of the school facilities for this. The other school was close enough to the church that we could walk the children to our church building. There was an advantage to holding class at the church building as this helped the students to identify with the church. It was also helpful for the teachers in setting up the classrooms. Eventually it was no longer permissible for us to use any school facilities for teaching Bible classes as this was seen as being unconstitutional, although we also saw it as another attempt by the Enemy to put a stop to this work.

The Tohatchi congregation had a little money set aside in savings and some of it was used to purchase a used school bus. The first bus was small and seated 32 passengers. Eventually a larger one was purchased that seated 66. From that time on, we transported the children from both of the boarding schools to the church building for weekly classes. Arrangements were also made with the public elementary school that we come one afternoon each week to pick up all students that had parental permission and take them to our Bible classes at church and then back home.

Understandably, all this teaching of Bible classes took a lot of our time each week. We saw it as an important way of outreach and of the planting of seeds of faith in the hearts of many children. For a large number of these children, this was the first contact they had ever had with Jesus and with the Word of God. Besides the actual teaching, there was the time needed to make lessons that were

Chapter Four: Tohatchi

suitable for the children in our situation. It always amazed us how well the children listened to the lessons from the Bible. The majority of them attended class regularly in spite of the lure of after-school sports events which we regularly seemed to be in competition with. I will never forget one of my classes of sixty boys, grades five and six. Those boys enjoyed the Bible stories immensely and raised the roof with their enthusiastic singing without the sort of bashfulness one might characterize that age group with. Helen usually taught a large class of girls and the smaller children were taught by one of the volunteers from the church or by the missionary interns who served with us at Tohatchi from time to time.

On Tuesday afternoons, after a few years of working in Tohatchi, Helen and I also taught a class of about 20 children in the home of one of our recent converts. This was in the community of Twin Lakes which was ten miles to the south. Our host did all the work of advertising the classes, but was not prepared to teach them herself as she was still too unfamiliar with the Bible. We provided light refreshments for the children each week, as we did with the children who attended Bible classes at the church. Besides Bible lessons, the children also learned a lot of songs and loved it. Similar classes were held in a couple of homes in the community of Mexican Springs, 7 miles to the southwest, but as there were other church members capable of doing that task, our help was not needed much other than making sure that the teachers had the necessary lesson materials.

We prayed often that the Lord would cause the small seeds that were planted in these children to grow into mighty followers of Christ. By reaching the children at an early age, we hoped the Gospel would be more able to take firm root in their lives with an eye toward the harvest in the many years ahead. In the meantime, such classes were a way by which to also reach parents of these children who otherwise might not have been immediately receptive to the message of the Gospel. In some cases, we have seen the fruition of our work already, but much of the harvest is yet to be gathered.

I asked Helen to tell more about this herself.

Chapter Four: Tohatchi

We taught a lot of children, and we did more of it in Tohatchi than anywhere else. Tohatchi was a town of many schools. I was in my element there.

Earlier, I had thought that, if we ever moved closer to where there was a college and where we were close to an elementary school, I would get my teacher's certificate updated and get into teaching full time again. In Tohatchi this would have been possible, but I began to see great opportunities for volunteer teaching in the church. I chose to do the latter. After all, people who can teach reading and math are easy to find, but it's harder to find someone who has been trained to teach the Bible and is willing to do so without pay.

There was another reason why I chose to teach Bible classes as a volunteer. I figured it would allow me to choose how much to get involved. I had discovered how enjoyable it was to raise teenagers and I wanted to do it well. But this took a lot of my time.

We taught children in three different categories. First, there were the government boarding school children. We taught them on weekdays after school and usually in our church building. These children presented the biggest challenge. They were needier in every way. They missed living in a family. Their Bible knowledge was minimal. They loved individual attention. Some of them had a tendency to run away from school when they got a chance. We were well aware that our taking them to the church building might provide a way for them to attempt such an escape to their homes.

These students were irregular in attendance, which made it difficult for us to build a lesson on the previous lesson. Yet we were able to get Christian principles into their hearts. This was because all people are hungry to know God's love. Also it was because God blessed our teaching efforts. For many it was the first time they would hear about Jesus.

The second category was the day school children. We also taught this group of children on a weekday after school. Most of these were from the public school, though a few attended the boarding schools during the day while living with families at home. These children were a lot like the average child that lives in any community anywhere. Many of them attended our church with their families. They were much easier to handle and the class sizes were smaller.

Then there were the Sunday school classes taught in our church on

Chapter Four: Tohatchi

Sunday mornings before the worship service. At one point in Tohatchi, we had four children's classes plus two classes for youth and two adult classes. This went on 52 Sundays a year.

On Sundays we used purchased materials, while on weekdays we used lessons which we ourselves had made. These included a teacher's guide and worksheets for three different age levels. With these homemade materials, we managed to cover all the main Bible stories in three years from September to May. We did our best to make these lessons directly applicable to the lives of the children.

I would sometimes give the children an opportunity to accept Jesus as their Savior, usually at the end of a story that was suitable for closing with an invitation. Whenever children responded, I usually put the other children to work with something and would talk and pray with the two or three that wanted to accept Christ.

You might wonder if these children knew what they were doing when they indicated a desire to follow Jesus. Did their commitments to Jesus stick? I could tell you many stories, but will share just one of them. When I was substitute teaching 4th grade at the Newcomb school (in our Toadlena days), there was a boy, whom I will call Tony, in my class. He gave me a hard time one day. I kept him in for recess to undo something he had done wrong. Imagine my surprise a few days later when Tony began coming to our Bible class held at the Newcomb church building every Tuesday afternoon. Someone must have invited him. Of all things, I happened to be teaching the fourth graders at Bible class that day, meaning he would be in my class.

We did our usual singing and then divided into our different classes. While I was teaching the Bible story, I felt the Lord telling me to give an invitation after I finished the story. I argued with myself, "I haven't planned for this. How can I tie this in with the lesson? It's too crowded in here, there's no private place to pray with them, and I really don't have time to do it anyway." But the Holy Spirit kept nudging me. So I explained to the class what it meant to ask Jesus to be their Savior. Then I asked all the children to close their eyes and asked them to raise their hand if they wanted to accept Jesus as their Savior.

I was surprised and pleased when Tony and one of the other boys raised their hands. There was no opportunity to meet privately with the two of them and so I explained again the way of salvation to the whole

Chapter Four: Tohatchi

class and asked the boys if they really wanted to ask Jesus into their hearts, to which they responded, "Yes." So I prayed the Sinner's Prayer with them with the boys repeating after me. Then class was dismissed.

There was little opportunity for follow-up as this was at the end of the school year and later that summer we moved from Toadlena to Tohatchi. Some years later, though, one of the Christian teachers from Newcomb told us about a teenage boy named Tony who came from a difficult home. The teacher said, "This boy is a Christian and I've been talking to him about living the Christian life." We talked a bit more and found out that it was the same Tony I had led to the Lord. God had remembered his commitment and had a teacher now, and perhaps others as well, to encourage him in the Christian life.

Over the years, Gary and I have met many other people who told us that they first heard about Jesus in one of our Bible classes at a school. Some have even told us how this eventually led to their conversion to the Christian faith.

--Helen Klumpenhower

The mission at Tohatchi suited us well. In a number of ways it was a less difficult work than what we had experienced in Toadlena. We experienced no major communication gap as more people had been given the privilege of attending school and learning English. Tohatchi was also less isolated and relatively close to the city of Gallup where there were job opportunities for the people. Most of the church families had jobs and this gave some regular income, even though most of the jobs were not high-paying. The people had learned to interact more with people other than from their own culture. It also helped that we ourselves had grown in confidence after the first seventeen years in ministry. Since our college days, we had learned a lot, mostly through trial and error. The ministry at Tohatchi felt like a long-lasting honeymoon that resulted from being a good match.

Our children eventually began to feel at home too. They were reaping the benefits of living close to school and having the opportunity to take part in after-school activities such as band and sports. They also enjoyed the church, especially when there was a large increase of youth at church. The church also provided other

Chapter Four: Tohatchi

activities, including a church softball team. On Sunday evenings, after the service, the team, which basically consisted of anyone who wanted to show up, practiced on the ball field close to church. Those who did not play on the team served as spectators and cheerleaders while they sat on the bleachers to enjoy each other's company and sip on a soda.

Jim and Mark had been given the option of attending Rehoboth Christian School which was a twice-daily 35 mile bus ride from home. They strongly preferred to attend school locally so that they could be home more often and take part in school activities more easily. We made it clear, however, that church meetings would have preference over sports activities except for special circumstances. The boys joined the high school basketball and track teams over time. This gave us a good opportunity to meet the community whenever we went to see a ball game. Helen joined booster clubs made up of parents who were interested in further supporting the school band and sports. It was a way of trying to make friends with the people in our community. In this way it was an advantage to have our children in the community school rather than in another community.

One of the high school students often followed our sons as they walked home from school. He wanted to be friends with them and had grown an appreciation for our family. He knew us from the Bible classes we held at the boarding schools where he had attended our classes. Many nights he stayed at our home and we enjoyed having the opportunity to minister to him. This young man came to making a commitment to Christ during this time. He was baptized and joined the church together with a group of fourteen others that included our son Mark.

In a few years' time, we had come to know a number of the staff at the schools, including the new high school principal with whom we had had several conversations. It bothered us that the walls in the school lobby were decorated with murals that depicted Navajo gods. In one of her conversations with the principal, Helen told him how we felt about those murals and that we were afraid of problems that could result by having depictions which represented an evil power on the walls. The principal listened politely, but since he was not a Christian, he was not aware of the danger of giving attention to demonic powers. The artwork was popular to many people and he saw no reason to remove the murals.

Tohatchi High School went through a terrible crisis around this time. In February of 1985, the same principal was having a difficult meeting with his superintendent at the central district office in Gallup where he was being asked to resign. While agitated, sitting there in the superintendent's office, the principal pulled out a gun he happened to have with him, shooting and killing the superintendent on the spot. He was charged with pre-meditated murder.

The entire community of Tohatchi, which was also the home of the superintendent, was completely stunned. The school staff and the students were in a total state of distress. The teachers gathered themselves into one room, still in shock. One of the aides, a member of our church, suggested that they ask me to meet with them. I therefore had the opportunity to pray with them and for them and to point them to the Lord's presence, even in such times as this.

The following morning, Helen and I went to Gallup to try to visit with the principal at the jail. We were permitted to visit him in his cell where he was surprised to see us. We had the time to point him to a new life in Jesus and we prayed with him. Our visit with him was much appreciated. Several months later he wrote Helen a letter from prison in which, among other things, he admitted, "You were right," referring to the murals at the school. Later, we noticed that the new administration at the school had the murals removed by repainting the wall. As for the principal, he became ordained as a minister in the Catholic Apostolic Church, even while serving out his life sentence.

A GROWING CHURCH

On October 10, 1985, our church had a special celebration as we commemorated seventy-five years since the dedication of the church building. This was a good opportunity to toot our horn in the community by holding three days of festivities to which everyone was invited. We felt it was a great success. We had a parade and there were 22 entries from the community. The church float gave thanks to God for the 75 years. People were lined up along the

Chapter Four: Tohatchi

Part of parade celebrating The 75th Anniversary of Tohatchi Church building

street to watch the parade. The whole community was invited for a dinner at the community chapter house where the men of the church had roasted a donated cow for the occasion. There was plenty to eat for everyone, as our church members were most generous with their food donations. We presented evening programs at the church where we shared the Lord's blessings over the years and presented the history of the church. Members put together a play in the Navajo language and setting depicting the experiences of the first missionaries visiting a Navajo home. This celebrative event helped the church become even more noticed in the community and brought more visitors to our Sunday services.

Members of the church were given some instruction on making visits in the community in order to share the gospel. While we were in Toadlena, we went to every house with the gospel message, but here we zeroed in on only those who had showed some interest in the Christian way. A couple of evenings were spent going out two by two visiting these potential members. Those who were unable to go out agreed to meet at church to pray for God to bless the visiting. At a certain time that evening, everyone met together at the church to report on the visits they had made. The response was positive.

One family that was visited requested that we instruct them in the Christian life immediately.

During one of the lessons we gave them a few weeks later, we were talking to them about God's forgiveness of our sin. The husband kept on asking the question, "Can we be absolutely sure that the Lord forgives us when we have repented of our sins?" We assured him by reading Bible verses with him. The husband showed great delight and thanked the Lord on his knees. At another meeting with the same family we explained clearly the good news of salvation through Jesus Christ as found in John 3:16. His wife said to us, "I've gone to the Catholic Church all my life but can't understand why nobody ever taught me these things before." This family became wonderful members of our church. He later served as elder in our church and was delegated to attend our denominational synod.

God's spirit was also at work in another family where we gave instruction. They shared how that they felt guilty about something they had done. For some time they had lived in a rented apartment in Albuquerque, and when they moved back to the reservation, they had taken with them the gas range that belonged with the apartment. The lady told us that she was filled with feelings of guilt whenever she was cooking food on the stove. We agreed that the wrong had to be corrected and the range had to be returned to its rightful owner. Since the couple was without transportation, I offered to take it back in the mission vehicle myself. To say the least, the owner was very surprised when he saw the gas range and was told the story. "I appreciate your bringing the range back to me," he said, "and I appreciate your honesty. But," he continued, "since I don't really need it anymore, why don't you just take it back with you so that family can continue to use it."

The councilman who represented the community of Coyote Canyon in Window Rock, the tribal headquarters, began to attend our church services together with his wife and teenage children. They asked if I would set aside one evening a week to instruct them in the Word of God. He was familiar with the Bible and the Christian faith since his father used to help out at church as an interpreter years earlier. This family also confessed Jesus as their

Chapter Four: Tohatchi

Savior and joined our church membership list.

With the addition of so many more families, the church was running out of adequate space for all. We were able to squeeze 150 people or more into the upstairs sanctuary, but there was not enough room in our fellowship room downstairs. The men of the church, therefore, decided to do some remodeling work in the fellowship room. In one corner there was a room that was never being used for anything. In the early years of the mission, the room was used as the place where missionaries prepared the bodies of the dead

Sunday morning service in Tohatchi Church.

for burial. Although this practice had long been discontinued, the room was never used for anything else because some people had uncomfortable feelings about using it. They preferred to stay out of that room and called it the "ch'íindii" or "ghost" room. The extreme avoidance of "ghosts" and other things associated with dead bodies was still a lingering result of being brought up in the traditional Navajo religion.

The men, however, decided to take out the wall and add the extra space to the fellowship room. Their loss of fear was evidence that they had matured in their Christian life. I pitched in to help with the remodeling project and enjoyed doing it even though I lost my good crow bar at that time. By mistake it probably ended up with the trash pile.

A secretary at the high school asked if we could baptize her son at our church. It was explained to her that we baptize only children of faithful believing parents. She would first have to receive Jesus as her Savior and Lord and we would assist her with instruction classes. After all that, we would consider the baptism of her son. Not only did this bring the lady to church, but her mother and siblings also. This was a family of eleven children and this certainly helped to fill the church sanctuary on Sundays. The mother, Liz Jones, was familiar with the Christian faith because she was a daughter of Walter Bitsie, who used to serve as a missionary assistant and interpreter at the Tohatchi church.

It was a joy to work with this family and to provide them with weekly instruction in the Christian faith. The children ranged greatly in age, with a number of them in their twenties, having already established families of their own, to a handful of teenagers and a few young, elementary school-aged girls. They all began coming to church at once, instantly bulging our attendance. It was quite a chore to get to know them all by name as, besides all looking somewhat alike, they all had a regular name and an unrelated nickname which was more commonly used. William, the oldest son, was known as "Buggy", Kenneth was called "Killer", and so on down the line. I had a hard time keeping Kenneth and his brother Kevin ("Jo-Jo") apart.

This wasn't too much of a problem though, until the Sunday when the Jones clan joined the church and were all baptized, except for two of them, in front of the entire congregation. As Kenneth came up to take his turn, I began to baptize him as "Kevin". Of course, he immediately corrected me and said, "I'm not Kevin! I'm Kenneth!" I started over again, making double sure of their correct names the rest of the way through.

The Joneses all lived in Mexican Springs. This family has become very influential in the church. Three of the boys have been serving on the church council and have demonstrated fine leadership ability. Helen and I always appreciated this family for being

Chapter Four: Tohatchi

generous to us and fun-loving. We have enjoyed many wonderful cookouts in their backyard by the grill, especially when there was a family wedding, birthday party, or a graduation party.

Mexican Springs Trading Post. Most small communities on the reservation have a trading post which serves as store and Post Office.

There was yet more growth to the church that came out of this extensive family. At one of our "Gospel Sundays", a specifically evangelical service we held from time to time, I brought a message on Noah and the flood. It was explained that, for Noah, there was only one way to escape the flood—the ark—just as Jesus is God's only way for us today. At the altar call at the conclusion of the service, a mother with her three small daughters came forward where she made a dedication to Christ. She was Liz Jones's sister, another daughter of Walter Bitsie. Her conversion had a great impact on herself and those around her. Now one of her desires would be to witness to her co-workers whenever they shared their problems with her during lunch breaks. On her desk she displayed a plaque that said, "Jesus Is My Friend." It became a conversation piece and often her co-workers asked her to pray for them as she witnessed to them.

As the church at Tohatchi continued to see numerical growth, so also there was spiritual growth and a maturing in the faith. There came a desire to become organized as an indigenous church that was governed by elders and deacons. Over the years, the missionary pastor had acted as the church leader with the input of a steering committee that was made up of some of the leading church members. This desire to become an indigenous church had surfaced years earlier in the 1920s, but had not fully materialized. Although our Navajo churches were sometimes criticized as having become too dependent and lacking a sense of responsibility, this was not true in all of the churches. Some of our churches were more mature than others and several were indicating a desire to rule themselves.

Consistory of Tohatchi Church

Several congregational meetings were set up where instruction was given to the whole church on matters such as the purpose of the church, the government of the church, the responsibilities of church members and the responsibilities of ministers, elders and deacons. This resulted in the Tohatchi mission becoming an "organized church" in 1984. In a special service, our first elders and deacons were installed to serve as its leaders. Although the church remained in need of financial assistance for the foreseeable future, it was now officially a church. Some of the other churches on the reservation also experienced progress and maturing and became "organized." Together these churches as a group became known as "Classis Red Mesa" which was carved out of the much larger "Classis Rocky Mountain". Classis Red Mesa is centered on the Navajo Reservation.

From the time I came to the Navajo Reservation to work in Toadlena, I served as an ordained evangelist while pastoring a church as well. My main work was that of missions and evangelism. I took the gospel message to those who did not know it and had not heard it, and to those who had heard, but did not believe. But now my work was changing, especially at Tohatchi. Less time was spent in sharing the gospel with unbelievers and I was mainly involved with feeding and maturing believers and equipping them for service. The congregation had reached the stage where it really needed a pastor rather than an evangelist.

Over the years, people approached me several times asking that I would consider the ordination of minister. One day, two couples from one of my supporting churches came to visit us. Their main purpose was to talk about my ordination. At first, I received this with little enthusiasm. It seemed to me that I was functioning perfectly fine and that the formality of an ordination would not change anything. I promised to do some serious praying and thinking about it though. As time went by, however, it became clearer that if I was called to serve as pastor of the church, I should also be willing to request ordination and have the backing and recognition from the denomination that supported me.

For the next year, I spent a lot of time in study. Some of this was done during long walks in the canyon where I could be all alone. Classis Red Mesa examined me and granted me the ordination as a minister. On June 1, 1986, it became official in a special worship service at the Tohatchi church. The elders of the church took a leading role in the service and they and the visiting pastor laid their hands on me. Suddenly, there was a clap of thunder. Although the sky was predominantly blue, there was a dark cloud above the church building that produced the thunder. I do not know what other people thought of this and did not ask them, but to me it seemed as if the Lord was showing His approval in that service. The ordination did not change me personally, but it felt good to know that I had done the right thing.

"TRY BINGO"

The Roman Catholic Church in the southwest had its roots in Mexico and was weak compared to the Catholic Church in other parts of the country. Unfortunately, they did not take a strong stand against non-Christian religions and had a tendency to mix pagan ideas into their religion. This was an attempt to be more attractive to the pagan world. Their teaching also stressed a salvation through the Church and the faithful adherence of rituals, rather than salvation only by faith in Jesus Christ. The Catholic Church in Zuni went so far as to cover the inside walls of the sanctuary with murals of the Zuni gods.

It was during the years of World War II that the Roman Catholics put up a church building in Tohatchi. Previously they had done most of their work in the southern part of the reservation which lies in Arizona. The Presbyterian Church was the dominant church in the northern part of the reservation in Arizona and the Christian Reformed Church was active mainly in New Mexico. We did not associate much with the Catholics even though their headquarters in Tohatchi was close to us—just over the hill to our north, in fact. They viewed *us* as bringers of another gospel and as an obstacle that stood in their way.

The main attraction at the Roman Catholic Church was their weekly Bingo games. This was actually a kind of glorified gambling that became popular as people had the opportunity to hit the jackpot and earn a few dollars quickly. A long line of automobiles could be seen driving up to their facilities each Wednesday evening as people hoped to strike it rich.

Not everyone in the Catholic Church was in agreement with what was going on there. One day, the three nuns who were on the staff came to visit with us, unbeknownst to the local priest. They wanted our take on certain questions about the Christian faith, ones they had apparently been wrestling with. For one, they asked, "Can

Chapter Four: Tohatchi

a true Christian be absolutely certain of his eternal salvation?" They also shared some of their frustrations with their own rigid church hierarchy and how they had no opportunity to give their personal opinions and suggestions for their church programs. "We do not know all those beautiful songs that we can hear your congregation singing, and we wish that we could have that kind of singing in our services too", they told us. They also appreciated the strong stand we were taking against false religions and were personally not in favor of Bingo in the church. This was significant to us since the Catholic Church has in many mission fields allowed for the Gospel to be compromised by traditional beliefs, as well as promoting gambling in the name of outreach. As they left, they asked that we not let the priest know of their visit with us as that could make things difficult for them.

A big change took place, however, when the main priest who had resided there for many years was given another assignment and moved on. A younger pastor took his place, one who was more open to us. He came to visit one day and asked why our church sanctuary was packed with worshipers on Sundays while they only had a few regular attendees. "What do you do to make them come?" he wondered. Perhaps he had the idea that we were handing out attendance awards or using some other sort of gimmick. We had previously been (falsely) accused of handing attendance awards out to children who attended the weekly Bible classes. We explained to him that our congregation came to worship because they were attracted by the preaching of God's word and the singing of hymns that praised the Lord. He had to agree that our singing was very impressive and beautiful as the sound carried over the hill and into the community.

Some time later, I returned the priest's visit where we talked a lot more. Among the topics that came up was that of church finances. He encouraged me to introduce Bingo games in our church as they had done. Those games alone brought in as much as $60,000 a year, an amount sufficient to the point that their church members were spared the need to give tithes and offerings. Although this was certainly more than our church was able to raise through tithing, we felt we did not need Bingo to raise money. We saw giving to the Lord as a privilege and felt honored to give in such a way. This seemed to puzzle him.

To my surprise, he asked me if our congregation could meet at their church on a Sunday evening to sing for them the songs they heard us sing on Sundays. He also asked if I would be willing to preach a message to them on John 3:16. According to him, we Protestant ministers were better trained to preach than he had been. I agreed to let him know after I had shared this request with my elders and deacons and upon their approval.

Approval was given and a terrific worship service was held at the Catholic Church a few weeks later with the building packed with people, most of them from our congregation. Our group sang several of the great gospel songs in both Navajo and English and it was my privilege to speak on John 3:16 as requested. The priest and his people were impressed and asked immediately for one more such meeting, possibly at our church facility. Again they asked us to sing gospel songs and to bring a message from God's Word. We accepted this request gladly and this resulted in a second meeting together. Our people brought plenty of food for a potluck dinner together. All in all, we were grateful for this fine opportunity to share the gospel of Christ.

SATAN'S SNARES

This is not to say that we were willing to hold religious services with all those who held just any and all beliefs. There were a number of times where we had to draw the line at standing side by side with those who preached something other than the true Gospel.

For example, there was to be a big dedication of a brand new gymnasium at the Tohatchi High School. This was a community event and, in order to please everyone, they asked the medicine man, the Catholic priest, Mormon elders, and me as a representative of a Protestant Church to take turns leading in prayer. I declined the offer and made it clear that we did not believe in mixing all kinds of religions together hoping that this would result in a good meeting.

At another time there was to be a dedication of a new stretch of highway and again they asked me to participate with a prayer while

Chapter Four: Tohatchi

the medicine man would have a chant to his gods and the Catholic priest would anoint the highway with holy oil. I declined again to participate. There came criticism for my refusal and for the strong stand I had taken. A number of people in the community regarded this as being anti-cultural and narrow-minded, but the vast majority of Christians in the community backed me up wholeheartedly.

The "Peyote" religion was strong in the Tohatchi community. This religion, the Native American Church, as it is called, was introduced to the Navajo by other native tribes during the 1930s. This religion advertised itself as the religion for all native people only. It had appeal in that it mixed religious beliefs—the traditional religion of the Navajo people and other Native American religions—and it even mixed in a few Christian teachings.

The peyote plant is similar to a cactus and brought in from Mexico. It is either boiled so that a person can drink the juice or else it is dried and smoked. The result is that the person has hallucinations. These hallucinations are believed to be visions from God as He communicated to you. They did not teach biblical truths, however. They taught that Christianity as preached in the church was for white people only. Any native who accepts the Christian faith was and is criticized as being anti-cultural. This religion was another one of Satan's ways to keep people in bondage to sin and without a true savior.

Someone shared her problems with Peyote with us. She had become a faithful Christian and had served the Lord for several years. While visiting her family in Arizona, her family had invited her to a Peyote meeting. Not willing to upset the family, she went along, but with no intention of taking part as she had heard that it was wrong to do so. According to her, she drank a little water, unaware that it was Peyote water. After that, whenever she wanted to read the Bible she was unable to see, and whenever she wanted to go to church meetings something would stand in her way to prevent her from doing so. She was deeply disturbed that she was no longer able to feel close to the Lord.

We prayed with her and asked Jesus to take away any evil powers that had possibly found an open door into her heart. She confessed to God that she had done wrong by attending a Peyote meeting and asked for the Lord's forgiveness. Her problems eventually disappeared and she was able to enjoy the Word of God again and also enjoyed worshipping Him in her home and at church.

Our community was also bothered with Satan worship. This was a growing trend mainly among young people. We noticed some activity at night on top of the mountain ridge south of our house. People claimed that the Satan worshippers had built an altar there where they sacrificed black cats to the devil. How much of this was actually true we will probably never know, but we became suspicious for we know how Satan works in many different ways trying to mislead people from the truth.

We were therefore quite wary of such activity as it might be found in the community. One day, someone came to our house asking me to come along to see a strange phenomenon. There was smoke coming out of the ground in the valley about a half mile away. They were wondering if this could possibly be evidence of devil-worship in progress. My pastor intern and I decided to go there and see for ourselves. I must confess that I had some fear in me, and as we went, I prayed that the Lord would protect us in case we would be confronted with some demonic activity.

As we came close to where the smoke came out of the ground, we heard the sound of what sounded like music blaring from a radio and we heard some talking. There were four high school boys there ditching school classes who had built a home for themselves in an arroyo. Their home was neatly covered with logs, branches, grass, and sand. Inside, the home was equipped with a few mattresses, blankets, some cooking utensils, and a small cooking stove with a chimney that went through the roof, making it appear as if smoke was coming out of the ground. It was actually a rather impressive setup. Surprised as we were by our discovery, they were even more surprised. We told the boys that it would be better for them not to skip school or otherwise we would have to notify the authorities of their whereabouts. I learned a lesson from all this that we should not try to look for devils in every possible place and to not give Satan so much attention.

Helen and I energetically continued the ministry at Tohatchi. As more people were coming into the church, they naturally

Chapter Four: Tohatchi

brought with them their struggle and old sinful habits that needed to be overcome. Many families were suffering from the effects of alcoholism. A few areas where help was needed were marital problems, alcohol abuse, and the dysfunction that alcoholism brings to all people. Beyond the little help we could offer the people, in many instances, they were in need of professional help.

A Christian organization in Gallup known as "Village of Hope" was organized for the purpose of helping those who were struggling with alcoholism and abuse. They volunteered to present lessons at our churches to help people understand better the problems of alcoholism and how to help its victims. This resulted in starting AA, Al-Anon, and Alateen meetings at our church. Eventually a young family with professional training in alcoholism was sent to Tohatchi to help our church and the other churches also. They began to use the currently unoccupied assistant house as a temporary office. This was a much needed ministry for which we were thankful.

I had innumerable opportunites to witness to those struggling with alcoholism myself. On one cold New Year's Eve when I had to take a quick trip into Gallup, I stopped to pick up a lone, wandering hitchhiker, as I often did, hoping for an opportunity to point him to the Lord. The man looked like a mess, and as he came into the vehicle, it was easy to detect the smell of alcohol. I asked him what kind of day he was having and that opened him up. He was having a rotten day as he had lost the keys of his pickup truck, gotten kicked around by his wife, and shoved out of the house by his sons. He also mentioned that he was in trouble with the law and that there was nobody who cared about his problems. I assured him that Jesus does care. This got me no response from him. It appeared that it would be fruitless to try to carry on a deep conversation, but I took one more stab at it, saying, "It looks like you won't be having a happy new year."

He turned to me in response asking, "Are you a preacher"? I answered that, yes, I was. He paused and said, "I think that I'm supposed to be a Catholic." I assumed this to be his way of saying that he preferred to be left alone and did not want my services. Here was an example of someone in so much need of help with his problems, both his addiction to alcohol and his spiritual blindness.

It was someone like this that Village of Hope could serve to make a great difference in their lives.

Sometimes people buy the stereotype that all Native American people are drunks. It is already well-documented that alcoholism is rampant on the reservations, but this is very unfortunate and unfair to the many who do not take alcoholic drinks. These people often are living with shame and feel deeply saddened as they see the negative effects that alcoholism brings to their people. Possibly there would be more empathy shown towards these hurting people if we had a better understanding of the causes of this problem. With God's help, they are all still potential gems Jesus wishes to gather for His kingdom. By seeing them through His love we can learn how to reach and heal them.

IN TIMES OF NEED

While in Tohatchi, I conducted more than twenty funeral services per year. Since we were the predominant church in the area, people often came to us in times of need. Most of these funerals were for non-Christian people. I saw these funerals as opportunities to bring the gospel of Jesus. The members of our church had organized what was called a "church choir" and they would make an attempt to sing gospel songs in the Navajo language at the funeral services. No formal training or technical singing ability was ever necessary to be in this group—just a heart for worship. The "church choir" also enjoyed singing at the retirement home in Gallup where most of the residents at the center were Navajo people. The whole congregation met there one evening per month to worship with the residents. Afterwards, our group had a time for fellowship and ate supper at one of the restaurants in Gallup.

I was sometimes asked to come to a home in order to pray for a sick person. One family asked if I would also anoint the sick person with oil for they had heard that this was done in Bible times. I went to the home and took with me a small bottle of olive oil. The grandfather of the family was sick and had been in poor health for many months. Members of the family had filled the house and all showed a deep concern for their grandfather.

Although some Christian missionaries put emphasis on

Chapter Four: Tohatchi

anointing the sick with oil, I had not done so primarily out of fear that this would be seen as a magic cure to obtain healing. People believed there was magic power in a medicine man's corn pollen or in the holy water or incense used by the Catholic priest. There was an opportunity to teach an important lesson to everyone present. I explained that the oil that I brought with me was not a magic cure with some magic power. The oil was a sign that reminds us and assures us of the love of Jesus. The healing would have to come from the Lord and we would pray to the Lord for He has the power to heal and would do so if this was His will. I anointed the man's head and we prayed together for God's grace to bring healing. The man apparently did recover eventually, but neither he nor his family, even then, was drawn to the Lord in faith, nor did they ever come to worship with us.

Someone else shared with me his concern for his sick horse. Afraid that his horse might die, he asked if I would pray to God for the horse. Curious as the request was, I was glad to do so and reminded the man that not only did the horse need help, but all people need God's help too. Two days later he told me that his horse had died. Although understandably disappointed, he did not appear to be angry at the Lord or even at me. I used this occasion to teach him that God does not always give what we want, but what we need. If His answer is "no", the Lord must have something better in mind for us.

One of our most elderly members, Freda Bitsie, the grandmother of one of our church families was in critical condition at the hospital. Her condition was rapidly deteriorating and the doctors gave up hope for her and disconnected the life support system. She was in a deep coma and, according to the doctors, it was just a matter of a few hours. I joined the family by her bedside and there was comfort in the fact that she had embraced the Christian faith and shared earlier that she was sure of her salvation. Together we thanked the Lord for her life of so many years and shared our desire that she stay with us for a few additional years. We confessed together that the Lord was almighty in power and able to restore her to health even in her poor condition if He wanted to do so. The family placed Freda into the Lord's hand after which

Chapter Four: Tohatchi

many of them, including myself, went home for the night.

The following morning a call came from the hospital that Freda had come out of her coma during the night and was responding. To the amazement of everyone, she was able to return home after a few days and was well. She lived one more year before the Lord took her into glory. During that last year of her life, she was a witness for the Lord to those who met with her. She kept her suitcase neatly packed with her best clothes as a reminder to all that she was ready to go to be with Jesus whenever He called her.

It was common for people to come to our house to ask for some food or money. These were people from all over the U.S. who traveled across the nation and stopped at churches and mission posts looking for handouts. Some of these people deserved our attention and we helped them as much as we could by offering them some food and a place to sleep and by directing them to a shelter in Gallup. Not all who came to the house deserved our help. One of them told me that he was extremely hungry and asked if we could give him some food to eat. I told him that I would gladly give him a sandwich as a start. As I turned to go back into the house he called out to me. "I'd like it on wheat bread and with ham and cheese on it." Well, this was enough indication to me that he could not be too terribly hungry, but rather out to take advantage of people. I told him, "You're not hungry. If you were, you'd gratefully accept whatever food I gave to you." I told him to leave. At that he became very angry and said that he was cursing me and the whole church by his gods. He muttered some strange words that I could not understand and turned and left.

There were occasions where we did feel that we should keep someone overnight, especially in the winter time when the temperature at times dipped to zero degrees or even lower. It was not uncommon every winter for people to die of exposure to the cold. In the basement of our house there was a small room with a bed where they could stay. To take strangers in like that was a little risky perhaps, but we were willing to take that risk. We did not have major problems with them except that on two occasions we heard someone in the bathroom during the night and by morning we found that they had used up all our rubbing alcohol and mouthwash

Chapter Four: Tohatchi

to satisfy their craving for alcohol. In each case, these people left the house early in the morning before we got up.

We also had to help some who were victims of abuse—young mothers with a few small children were desperate for a place to stay. We were thankful to the Lord that we were able to reach out to them and minister to them in Jesus' name and then refer them to a safehouse in Gallup where they would be cared for.

THE NEXT GENERATION

The congregation at Tohatchi had always attracted many children and youth. This kept us all very busy and demanded perhaps the largest bulk of our time. Not only were there weekly Bible classes to conduct, but we also put on a number of Vacation Bible School programs in the summers.

Margie Silver teaches VBS in Tohatchi.

VBS kept us occupied for about one month. We usually held four separate Bible schools in the area. The one at Tohatchi was the largest with about 80 children in attendance. At Mexican Springs, the classes were held in the community chapter house where about 60 children attended. A third class was in the community of Twin Lakes where a family made a place for us to meet with 30 children attending. The fourth was held in Coyote Canyon, at first at the chapter house and later at the home of the councilman who had become a member of our church. He let us use a nice shade house outside and a large hay barn where the children could sit on hay bales. We usually attracted 40 or more children there.

The church bus was used to transport many of the children, but in places where the roads were too rough for the bus, the parents had to bring the children themselves. Also, we used a few vehicles donated by church members. Much of the teaching was done by members of the church which we strongly encouraged so that the church members would get experience and learn through it. Some who were not ready to serve as teachers were used as assistants in the classrooms, drivers, playground supervisors, or refreshment servers.

Each VBS ended after one week with a closing program for parents and friends. At Coyote Canyon, a closing program was usually scheduled for a Sunday evening when the whole Tohatchi Church could attend and present a potluck supper for the children and their parents. It was rewarding to hear the children sing and share some of the Bible verses they had learned. These programs drew a nice crowd of people and gave us an opportunity to reach out to families and to invite them to come and worship with us.

As with the weekday Bible classes, the VBS at Mexican Springs was run by the Christians in that area and did not need much help from Helen and myself except, again, that we made sure they had the necessary teaching materials. The Christians at Mexican Springs were eager to reach out into their community with the gospel. They had a desire to have their own church building in their community rather than to worship at Tohatchi. This seemed good to everyone, so the group went to work on it. The community chapter gave its approval to the idea. One family set aside a piece of land at a good location next to the main road. After a load of required paperwork was completed, the Tribal government also gave its approval for the building. However, despite all this effort, towards the end, the group at Mexican Springs felt that they were not quite ready to be on their own. They preferred to stay with the Tohatchi church and did so. Still, this desire for expanding God's kingdom was a positive sign of maturing in our church.

Chapter Four: Tohatchi

Tonya Jones attends VBS in Mexican Springs.

Over the years, the Vacation Bible School did have some positive results. The Lord used it as one of a variety of ways to bring people to faith in Christ. We have often been stopped by people who told us that they had attended our classes. A young woman introduced herself and her mother to us one day and said, "I used to be in your Bible school in the hay barn at Coyote Canyon. During one of those times in the barn, I gave myself to Jesus." Later she encouraged her mother to take her to a Christian church to worship Jesus with her there. They later became full members of the church at Rehoboth. Others have told us similar stories how that over the years they always remembered the Bible stories we had taught them either at Vacation Bible School in the summer or Bible classes for the school children during the school year. With the grace of God, these planted seeds remained alive.

Some of the younger couples in the church indicated that they would be willing to serve as leaders of a youth group. This was a good thing since, even though we were fully aware of the need for a youth program, we did not have enough time to be involved in it. This youth group had the potential of evolving into a large ministry. Before long, the group numbered around twenty-five and it became

Chapter Four: Tohatchi

necessary to split the group into older and younger.

The youth came to meetings for a Bible lesson and for games and other fun. They attended meetings with youth from other churches and crusades such as a Billy Graham crusade. They organized a softball team and played against teams from other churches. They had campouts on the mountain for spiritual retreats either alone or together with the youth of another church. One of the leading couples were teachers at the public school at Tohatchi who had come there from North Dakota and joined our church membership. It was a blessing to have a few teachers from our local schools join in our church program and they were well received and fit in well, even though many of them were not Navajo.

One evening I had to give a helping hand with transporting the youth home. My last passenger lived several miles into the countryside where I was not familiar with the many trails. On my way back, I lost my way home in the dark. Suddenly I found myself in the loose sand of one of the arroyos. The wheels began to spin and the engine stopped. After I asked the Lord to help me so far from any home or available help, the vehicle started up again and I managed to get out of the sand pit without any problems. I found my way home and had experienced the goodness of the Lord again.

Our church received a letter from Houston, British Columbia. We were curious and wondered who knew about us so far away. It was a request on behalf of a Christian church in Houston for some help from our youth. They were looking for native Christian youth who would be willing to help in leading a Christian youth camp for native people in their area. The Navajo were considered to be closely related to them through a common centuries-old heritage. This information was shared with our senior youth group. Four of those, two men and two women, volunteered to give six weeks of their time to serve.

The whole youth group became involved in raising money to help cover the expense of such a venture. They went around collecting a variety of items that would sell flea market-style in a busy Gallup parking lot, a much more effective way of running a profitable yard sale in the area. It could also be more adventurous. Among the items they sold were some of my pigeons and chickens.

Chapter Four: Tohatchi

Tohatchi youth raise funds at Gallup Flea Market. (Left to right) Mark Klumpenhower, Eric Tsosie, Jason Begay, Ferlin Manuelito

My birds usually sold pretty well in such places. Unfortunately, the youth were not as accustomed to handling the birds, especially the high-energy banty rooster I gave them to sell. The rooster managed to escape at one point, finally finding sanctuary by scuttling under, up, and somehow into the trunk of a car in the parking lot. Imagine one customer's surprise to find a group of youth waiting for him to tell him he had a live chicken in his trunk.

Thanks to the help from the Houston church, the necessary funds were raised and the four youth were put on the plane to Vancouver and from there into northern BC. It was a new undertaking for them, but each one enjoyed the experience a great deal. Being Native Americans themselves proved to be an advantage when they shared the gospel with people at the camp, even though they were of a different native tribe. When they made visits with the native tribe in that area, the people were delighted with their visit and treated them to moose steak and smoked salmon.

After six weeks, the four returned home and were greeted with a "Welcome Home" potluck dinner from the congregation. They shared their experiences and showed many slide pictures they had taken. One of the two young men who went proudly told how he had learned to spear salmon in the river and he had even caught one. They had been surprised that a few words of the language spoken were very similar to the Navajo language and it was an indication to them that the two tribes truly were distantly related to each other. The diet on which they had lived in BC was different from back home and each one had become hungry for roasted mutton and fry bread. In return, the church in Houston reported that our youth had done excellent work as representatives of Christ and were very pleased with them. In the end, it was a valuable growing experience for some of the youth of our church.

Most of the older youth at our church attended Tohatchi High School. They were instrumental in having the school request that our church would host the annual baccalaureate service and make up a program. We did this for three years, after which the school discontinued the practice. While it lasted, it was a great opportunity to speak to the whole community and especially to the younger generations.

The youth also set the stage for several church weddings. It was wonderful to see couples joined together in the Lord. It was my policy that I would not perform a wedding unless a couple completed some pre-marital counseling sessions and were in agreement with what was taught.

Church weddings had a lot of appeal. It was common for the bridal party to dress in traditional Navajo clothing which we always admired for the beautiful colors. But others splurged to rent gowns and tuxedos for the occasion or had the gowns specially made by someone. People also enjoyed the traditional American large wedding party including flower girls and ring bearers.

It was particularly important that a rehearsal be held here where knowledge of traditions such as these could not simply be taken for granted. I generally conducted rehearsals, as well as the weddings. At the rehearsal, it was common for some of the bridal party to be absent and we took that in stride. At one of the rehearsals, the whole wedding party was there except for the bridegroom who felt that he had too much else to do. That would not do. I told the bride, "Get him to this rehearsal or there will be no wedding tomorrow." She found him, he did come, and the wedding went on as planned.

Another young couple asked me to officiate at their wedding. They were from the community of Toyee where they attended a very small church. They completed the counseling sessions and we made the wedding arrangements. The couple told me that it would be the first Christian wedding in their little church building and that their congregation was eagerly anticipating the special event. The congregation decided to do some last minute repair work and painting on the building prior to the wedding.

When Helen and I arrived there on Friday evening for the wedding rehearsal, as planned, the people were all still working hard at making the building repairs. Some were painting the walls and others were plastering the ceiling. A blaring radio was providing some entertainment. Everyone was working hard, some even told us that they would work all night to be certain that everything would be ready for the wedding the following morning.

It was rather apparent that we could not have a typical rehearsal. We might barely pull off the wedding for that matter. With no other option, we simply held the rehearsal outside behind the building in the sand and the weeds.

We returned the following morning for the wedding which had been scheduled for ten o'clock. The remodeling work was not done yet, but it was close. It was then nine o'clock. After we waited for an hour, everyone stopped with their work, climbed off their ladders and took a seat wherever they could. The paint was still wet and the smell of it was overpowering, but we still had a nice Christian wedding in that little church. The ceremony was followed with a feast—outdoors. Of course, as the pastor, I was expected to wear my best suit for the occasion—the guests were mostly garbed in work clothes. When I got home, I checked for paint spots, but, fortunately, there were none. My pants had gotten somewhat dusty, however.

Chapter Four: Tohatchi

GEMS

We admired the members of our church at Tohatchi for the fact that so many of them were willing to take an active part in the life of the congregation. Some of them made visits to encourage the elderly and the sick. Others were willing to serve as teachers on Sundays, during the week, and at VBS in the summer. Those who were involved with teaching in the church took off from their regular jobs if possible to attend a Sunday school convention in Denver each year in February. Members of Second Christian Reformed Church of Denver showed a lot of hospitality by volunteering to have our people stay in their homes and by feeding them. This saved our people a lot of expense making it more affordable for them to attend. A few of our men who were leaders in the church were able and willing to bring a message in church when necessary or to speak at the retirement home whenever we held a service there. Still others faithfully helped with making repairs on the church buildings or vehicles. Some of these gems are going to be mentioned specifically as they have a story to be shared:

Robert and Dorothy Bowman were a couple who demonstrated faithfulness. They took part in practically all meetings at church. When we arrived in Tohatchi, we learned that Dorothy had served as Sunday school teacher for over thirty years without ever having been replaced. That probably qualifies her for some sort of record somewhere.

Edgar and Gladys Bitsoie were well known for their generosity. He was the "Barnabas" in the congregation—one known for encouragement—and demonstrated understanding and wisdom as an elder in the church.

Everett and Martha Manuelito were among the most dependable helpers we had. He was a great repairman and they both took time to teach Bible lessons in homes to families that requested it.

We were sure to see Ada Bitsie, one of our elderly members, every Sunday morning. When she was a young girl of fifteen, she was feeding a lamb from a bottle in a corral with other sheep and some goats. As she was bent over, the billy goat attacked and hit her in the head, causing the blindness she would have for the rest of

Chapter Four: Tohatchi

her life. Ada never complained about her fate and loved the Lord regardless, faithfully attending services well into her eighties. She was a model Christian to everyone.

Jane and Leo Bitsie

Leo and Jane Bitsie were another older couple who were very faithful in service to the Lord. For years he came to church very early on Sunday mornings to start up the coal furnace and ring the church bell. In spite of much tragedy and death in their family, they remained cheerful and were always ready to help out with the work. Jane called me "shiyaazh" (my son) and I have always regarded this as quite an honor. She had been a long time believer, having accepted Christ while attending a Boarding school and a Bible class there, much like the ones we conducted regularly. Jane was often a teacher in these classes and at VBS, giving back to the Lord in the same way as He had initially reached her. Leo would be there too, helping out in any way needed.

We also treasured James and Velma Nahkai. James attended a Methodist boarding school as a child and Velma attended school in Rehoboth. Their training in Christianity was a great help to the Tohatchi church. James was called into the service of our country in

World War II against Japan, serving as a Navajo Code Talker. He also survived the Bataan Death March in the Philippines. After the war, he became involved in the Navajo government serving as a councilman for the Tohatchi Chapter. He was respected for his strong stand for Christ and our church appreciated this couple for their generosity and humility.

There are other faithful members in the church and newer members who brought new life into the church and deserve mention here. In no way can we mention them all by name, however, but we want to honor them nevertheless. The Lord will honor them in His own way in time.

FUN AND RELAXATION

After graduating from high school, each of our sons except for the oldest attended the University of New Mexico in Albuquerque. There they met a student from East Germany who became a roommate to two of the boys. On several occasions, they invited him to visit us for a long weekend. As a young boy, he had always dreamed about going to America to see real cowboys, and here he was—staying among the natives of the American West.

The communist government refused him permission to study overseas and so he made an attempt to escape across the border into Hungary. He was captured and He spent the next three years in prison camp for re-indoctrination into communism, an altogether fruitless crusade on their part. The government of West Germany purchased his freedom and he was permitted access into West Germany and eventually from there to America.

The fall of communism in East Germany a few years later was a great event for this young man. Upon hearing that the Berlin wall had been broken down, he made a trip back to see for himself and to visit with his parents who were still in East Germany. When he finally returned to America, he presented me with a piece of the Berlin wall. As a rock collector, I prized this "rock" but so did our son Jim, who as a history teacher has used it as visible evidence of the fall of communism.

Our son Jim was married on New Year's Eve in 1990 in Albuquerque. His older brother David was married the following year

Chapter Four: Tohatchi

in Tohatchi with a reception at the Tohatchi Chapter House. Both sons married Christian women, which we were deeply grateful for.

The work at Tohatchi, with all the teaching and visiting and the pastoral work, demanded a lot of time and energy. With the good health that we both enjoyed, it was possible to carry a heavy load. The experience we had gained over the years, combined with an increase in confidence and knowledge, was very helpful in the work and made it easier in some ways. Both of us made sure to take time off to relax.

Our weekly day off was Fridays, unless there was a situation where I had to be present. We made a point of going into Gallup to do shopping and sometimes to eat out. I enjoyed going fishing in some of the lakes higher up the mountain while Helen preferred to stay home to read books.

Even from the beginning of our time out west, during our annual vacation time, we drove cross-country to see the land and meet with relatives and friends. When the children were still small, we all went together on vacation, providing us with valuable family time. In later years, we tried to reserve one week for the family to go camping and fishing at Navajo Lake State Park and enjoyed that as well. Helen and I even continued to do so after the boys were no longer living at home. For about twenty years we enjoyed the used pop-up camper that we bought and it gave us a lot of camping enjoyment. We also used it at the Cottonwood Pass Bible Conference we had in the mountains each summer.

Regular walks into the canyon behind the house gave me some necessary relaxation. I had the habit of picking up small shiny stones of all different colors when I went walking in the canyon. I used these during the winter months for my stonework hobby as I carefully glued the stones on lamps or pottery or vases.

On walks in the canyon there was an opportunity to observe the marvels of God's creation. There were horses, coyotes, foxes, jackrabbits and many different birds, including an occasional bald eagle. One day, when my brother-in-law was with me, we saw a cougar that was crouching towards a flock of sheep. When the cougar heard us, it suddenly disappeared among the many rocks and evergreen shrubs. A multitude of hummingbirds would gather in

Chapter Four: Tohatchi

certain areas to feed on desert flowers. I found myself in a swarm of hummingbirds on a few occasions. There were hundreds of them and they had no fear. I was able to come so close that it was almost possible to catch them in my hand. When I wore a brightly colored shirt, they landed right on me and it felt as if I was in paradise. Another day, I was walking among the flowering yucca plants and stopped to smell them and to admire their great beauty. As I held one of those flowers and held it over my eye, I saw a beauty that I had not seen before. There had been a few discouragements in the ministry and this resulted in my feeling somewhat gloomy. The beauty I saw inside that flower that day lifted my spirits and reminded me clearly of the Lord's presence.

Even at such times, the Lord's work seemed to find me. While resting on a large, flat rock in the canyon one day, I noticed a man coming down the steep mountainside and heading straight toward me. I waited for him and, as he came closer, I recognized him as a young man in our community. He asked if I had time to talk with him. As he sat next to me, the man shared all his hurts and problems and told me that he needed Jesus. Before he left, he repented to the Lord of his sins and asked Jesus to be his Savior. For several years, he did attend meetings at church and he was later baptized. Unfortunately, later he fell back into his old sins and he forsook the Lord.

Another way I enjoyed spending a day off was when I went to sell my extra birds at the flea market in Gallup where some of the vendors knew me as the "pigeon man". Not only was the flea market a good place to sell my birds, but I met a lot of people who recognized me and stopped by for a chat. One day, I presented Helen with a beautiful necklace of turquoise stones which someone asked me to trade for two pigeons.

Growing up on the rural reservation for the majority of their lives, our sons found their own ways to entertain themselves. My son, Mark, wrote the following concerning that aspect of their lives:

Having now lived as many years of my life off of the Navajo Reservation as on it, I understand now, even better than I did then, just how different my experiences have been compared to practically

143

Chapter Four: Tohatchi

everyone else I know in my cosmopolitan life today. I regard it today as an incredible blessing to not only have grown up in a family full of love, faith, and grace, but to have done so immersed in a different culture, in a place so remote and removed from many of the world's more shallow distractions.

I don't remember wanting or needing a whole lot of toys or material possessions growing up, or even now, for that matter. It probably helped only getting two channels with unpredictable reception on the black and white TV set we had—less commercials to tell us what we didn't know we were missing. It's not that we were so utterly unaware of the material world around us—we just didn't fixate on it. We already had what we needed. The land was our playground and our own imaginations grew fertile in the freedom one has when the outside world is not there to crowd it out with its regimented codes and fads.

My life today, however, revolves mostly around city folk raised in mainstream American suburbia, many of whom cannot fathom how a child growing up with such a scarcity of material distractions could do anything but go crazy from lack of entertainment. In this, I do not think my or my brothers' experiences are all that different from any other children who grew up in rural society. True, boredom has always been a distinct possibility for many young people with rural backgrounds, but we seemed relatively immune to it in our family. While so many others seemed to search for pleasure by escaping into the city, or, in their own despair, perhaps drowning themselves in alcohol, we learned to draw into each other as a family. When left alone, we learned to create our own entertainment. "Boredom" wasn't really much in our vocabulary.

One of my favorite things to do was to run around and explore the hills and canyons just past our back fences. This was true in both Toadlena and Tohatchi. I may not have had a mall anywhere near me, as I sometimes tell people, but not everyone has an open mountain range just beyond his backyard. Many people wouldn't probably find our landscape all that wonderful to run around in, dry and dusty most of the time, but it was all home to me. These quiet wanderings of mine brought out in me a certain creativity and sense of self, as well as great appreciation for the subtlety of God's creation. I learned to appreciate what little rain we got; the land really came to life in July and August when the rains came to suddenly reveal an otherwise dormant greenness

Chapter Four: Tohatchi

in the land. In some ways, the desert landscape we lived in provided a good metaphor for life on the reservation; just as the summer rains brought out an otherwise concealed beauty around us, the lack of diversions in our lives only accentuated the positive things we had been given all along.

We certainly could be creative—particularly Jack, whom most of our activities, more so in the early years, revolved around. He was behind the creation of a fictional town (populated by our toys), a TV network, game shows, stories, a live-stage rendition of "The Gong Show" (again, featuring our toy animals), and even the Chinese-American Baseball All-Star games. In this baseball series, he came up with names himself and we played out the games ourselves—well, sort of—in the backyard.

Over time, we would all develop our own creative skills in a variety of ways. One of the more memorable events put on by my older brothers and one of their friends was the "Toadlena 005"—a 5-lap bike race around the BIA boarding school. Every kid in town was invited who had a bike, and nearly all of them showed up. Jack created his own makeshift trophies both of the years the event was run. We joked that our area was so devoid of entertainment that that little event should have bumped off some of the other drivel from our local TV newscast's sports stories.

There were some "real" sports to be involved in, especially once we moved to Tohatchi. Here, Jim and I especially were able to compete in school activities such as basketball, track and field, and cross-country. It was also easier to be part of the school band. With greater time for school activities, it was also a bit easier to make friends.

Still, even all this could have been tiresome had it not been that we as a family managed to get away a few times a year. In the Toadlena days, it was sometimes as simple as doing an overnight in Farmington in a motel (Incredible luxury—color TV and 4 channels!). Once a year, we went into Albuquerque to do Christmas shopping for a weekend, my only experience with large-scale shopping centers until I was ten. One week in July was spent camping at Cottonwood Pass Bible Conference, a week-long retreat of all the CRC churches in the mountains. Eventually, with the purchase of a small tent trailer, we also camped a few times at Navajo Lake near Farmington for a week. We boys were teens or preteens by then, all of us growing quite tall, and only twice did we actually go

Chapter Four: Tohatchi

camping in the trailer as a whole family. Officially, it slept 7, though Jack quipped that that must be referring to the 7 dwarfs. The need for such outings dwindled by the time we moved to Tohatchi, though, as there were more activities to be involved with there, and the "city", Gallup, and the relative luxuries it afforded, was nearer.

Perhaps the greatest recreation we had as a family, though, was our (almost) annual family vacation when we usually traveled to Canada and/or Michigan to see relatives. Vacations were terrific on a number of levels. We spent a lot of quality time together and we rarely fought or bickered with each other. We got to see relatives we would hardly ever see otherwise. Going by car, we got to see the country and appreciate its diversity (if that word can be fairly attributed to Nebraska). Finally, we got to experience a world outside of the only one we really knew. For myself, it whetted a desire to explore my world even further, eventually leading me into a career teaching Geography. Still, my roots are grounded in my growing up on the reservation and the faith which was first planted there.

I have few to no regrets about growing up where I did. If I did have any, though, it was not, as many would suppose, for lack of fun, excitement, or other pleasures to fill me with. I was quite rich in all those things. My experiences growing up were full of the sorts of things that persevere through one's life: Imagination, wonder, and spiritual depth; appreciation of family, nature, and what you have over what you don't; and appreciation of God's constant provision, bringing rain, one way or another, into the desert.

Mark Klumpenhower

The church planned for a Labor Day retreat on the mountain with overnight camping for everyone. We set up camp near a spring where there was water. Nearby was a sheep dip where in the spring the people met together to dip their sheep in order to rid them of ticks and disease.

Most of the people slept in the back of their pickup trucks but a few had a camper or a tent to sleep in. Some slept out in the open in a sleeping bag and close to the fire pit to stay warm. We were parked in a circle so that it looked like an old fashioned wagon train with a group of pioneers. This retreat was a wonderful time of fellowship together with devotions, singing, eating together, drinking coffee and playing games. The cool mountain air gave us a good night's sleep, even when we could hear the hooting of an owl or the occasional cry of the coyote.

WELLANDPORT

After about ten years at Tohatchi, Helen and I felt that we needed a break from mission work. By now, all of our sons were on their own or off to college. We were both beginning to feel tired and overworked, even though we still enjoyed it. We therefore asked the mission board if we could have a leave of absence for one year while I would make myself available to serve as an interim pastor somewhere away from the reservation. The request was granted and this led to a ministry for us at the Christian Reformed Church in Wellandport, Ontario for the calendar year 1993. The elders of the Tohatchi church were willing to take on the challenge of taking care of the congregation as leaders and pastors during my absence. They wanted to be assured that, the Lord willing, we would return to join them again in the Tohatchi ministry.

The church at Wellandport made the suggestion that we come and visit them for a weekend so that we could meet each other. This seemed like a good idea, so we went by airplane to Buffalo, NY where one of the church couples picked us up and took us to Wellandport. The people received us warmly and we enjoyed visiting with several families. I led the worship services that Sunday. They then asked us officially to minister to them for the period of one year from January 1 through December 31 of that same year.

Towards the end of 1992, we packed our little pickup truck full of items we would need and headed for a cozy little house which the Wellandport church had rented for us and furnished with plenty of furniture and other household items. The living room looked like a flower shop, full of potted plants and flowers. People stopped by the house to welcome us and to check to see if we had need of anything.

It took a few weeks to become adjusted to a church that was quite different from the churches we were used to. In place of piano or guitar music, they were used to singing with a loud pipe organ. The form of worship was much more formal than we were used to having and the minister was expected to lead every part

Chapter Four: Tohatchi

of the worship service. They were not accustomed to having a special musical number or a testimony in their worship service. The services began exactly on time and were to be done promptly some 65 minutes later. The church adhered strictly to some old CRC traditions and followed them carefully, while on Navajoland we were much more informal.

People called me by the title of "reverend" and showed respect because of the work to which I had been called. In the Navajo churches we "earned" our respect and that seemed to make more sense to me. The churches in the Wellandport area took very good care of their pastors, but also expected them to perform well as they were held to a high standard.

As an interim pastor, my work was basically that of preaching, visiting, and general pastoral care. The church elders assisted with the pastoral care in the congregation. I had much more time on my hands than I had in Tohatchi. It was good to have more time to work on preparing sermons, and the lighter load also meant there was more opportunity to relax and do things for fun. This church was blessed with so much leadership. The various church groups and committees were functioning well without the need for a pastor's assistance. The pastor's wife was not needed to supervise the Sunday school classes or the work in the church kitchen. The church even had a custodian who kept the church spotlessly clean. This was a profound change for us.

But, as in all churches, there were problems in this church also. The year before we came, the church split into two groups over the issue of the ordination of women serving as elders and pastors. This split caused a lot of hard feelings among church members and even among family members. It was unfortunate that the church split resulted in having two separate denominations. There was a great need for reconciliation and love in the church and this could best be accomplished by solid Bible preaching with the emphasis on the love of God and with family visiting where people could air their feelings. The Lord was good and blessed our ministry there.

Interestingly enough, even here, back in my home province, I found myself in a place of ministering to a person of native heritage. It was a special joy to have this opportunity to instruct a Chippewa woman in the Christian faith. She had grown up on the Six Nations Reserve in Ontario. Several times she made the comment to me, "I can tell that you've been ministering to Native Americans because you understand me." The Holy Spirit worked in her heart and she was baptized and joined the membership of the Wellandport church. Her stories of her own native people reminded me of the same problems we faced on Navajoland, although I actually felt that their problems and their living conditions were even worse than we saw on the Navajo reservation.

The famous Niagara Falls was about thirty miles from home. It was nice to see and provided us with a good place to take visitors or our own children when they came to visit us. My parents and most of my siblings were living in Ontario and we visited them regularly as I had half a Sunday off each month. This gave me a long weekend to be away.

It was a particular blessing to us to spend 1993 in Ontario since my father was on his deathbed and passed into glory on May 5 of that year. We had ample opportunity to pay him visits that would have been impossible had we been on the reservation. The Lord must have planned our stay in Wellandport that year so we could be with loved ones at a time when we needed each other.

The year went by quickly, and before long we began to think about returning home to Tohatchi. The Wellandport church asked us to stay on, but we knew that the Lord wanted us back to the work to which we had been called. One of the staff members of the mission board asked, "Are you sure you want to go back there?" I answered that both Helen and I were sure and that our desire was to spend the final eight years remaining of our ministry until my official retirement working among the Navajo, if the Lord willed it. After retirement, we would be open to serve the Lord in another capacity and in other places. On January 2nd, 1994, we were headed back to Tohatchi, filled with happy memories from the past year. The Wellandport church gave us a special farewell to which they also invited my siblings.

To be away from our regular work for a year was, in our opinion, a very good thing for us, and we would encourage others to do the same if they needed a break. It was not just a learning experience for us as we ministered in a different culture and to different people in God's Kingdom, but we also had a renewed appreciation for the many positive things in our churches on Navajoland. It helped us to look at the work in Tohatchi from a new perspective and with renewed energy. It was also rewarding to see how the Tohatchi elders had been able to carry on without our presence. That was proof of a maturing there that we had hoped to achieve.

MOVING ON

It was early on an afternoon when we drove up to our house in Tohatchi again. While we were busy unloading the truck, we noticed several cars in the church parking lot, a number which increased as the afternoon went by. Although we surmised that there was some meeting taking place, we didn't know any specifics until they told us to join them—for a surprise Welcome Home potluck. We did a lot of catching up and did our best to give a report of our year spent in Wellandport. Everyone seemed pleased that we had been used by the Lord to lead a Chippewa woman to faith in Christ. One of the elders commented, "This must be why the Lord wanted you to go there for one year."

It felt good to be back in our own parsonage. Our son David and his wife Claire had lived in the parsonage part of the time that we were gone. David had a job transfer to Gallup and they were looking for a home. The Tohatchi church offered that they stay in the parsonage to take care of things. Then, at the same time, they could help out at church, although some people assumed that David would do some pastoral work during our absence. Still, it worked out well.

Within a few days, we were back at work and picked up the old routine of pastoring, teaching, and preaching. Unfortunately, this also meant I had to drive the big church bus again to take school children to Bible classes. It was a big responsibility to transport those loads of precious children every week while having to cross a busy highway. We prayed a lot that the Lord would grant us safety and that the bus would continue to run well. Some years earlier we had had a scare with the first bus when one of the front wheels came off just as I had finished crossing a narrow bridge.

Chapter Four: Tohatchi

Providentially, I was on a very rough piece of road and going less than 5 mph when it happened, so no one was hurt. It was always a relief for me to have all children safely back at their homes or at the school again.

The older boys at times could be somewhat rowdy and disobedient on the bus. They reminded me of the days when I used to travel by school bus myself. We were not always so well behaved either. Naturally, they were excited to get away from the school for an hour and from all the school rules. The boys had started the habit of, when exiting the bus, grabbing the ledge above the door and swinging out instead of walking. I kept warning them not to do it as someone might get hurt, but it was to no avail. Not liking to be blown off like that, I decided to do something about it. In the old barn, there was a can of roofing tar and the idea came to me to smear a thick layer of tar on the ledge over the bus door hoping that this would discourage the boys from swinging out.

The next time the children were let off the bus, I made a point of clearly reminding the boys again not to swing out. Not aware of the tar, they all one by one defied my warning by swinging out again. I could hardly keep my composure when the boys were walking towards their dormitory looking at their hands and wondering where all that tar had come from. I suppose they learned their lesson as they did not swing out of the bus any more after that. None of them ever talked to me about it, knowing that I'd have responded with an, "I told you so."

Over the years, the job of teaching so many children each week did begin to have its toll on us. As we were getting older, it became harder, but we continued with this planting of seeds as long as we were able to do so and as long as the Lord gave us the opportunity to do it.

A pastoral visit was to be made to a couple that lived 25 miles away and far into the countryside. It was much rarer these days for me to do visits at camps like this. It took a long time to get there for it had rained and the trails were very muddy and hard to drive on. It was no wonder that the family was surprised to see me at their home, but they were delighted that I had come.

The family had just finished butchering a sheep and was eager

Chapter Four: Tohatchi

to share some of the delicacies with me. Knowing that I ate all parts of a sheep, the lady fried a large pan filled with some of the internal organs and intestines. She gave me a plate and offered thanks to the Lord. She then presented the whole pan full of goodies for me to eat. I was told that this was all to be for me for they had already eaten. I accepted the food gratefully together with a large mug of black coffee and dug in. It reminded me of my days of campwork, a time which seemed to have long since passed into a more modern world. Wonderful and delicious as it was, though, on the way home, it felt as if there was a rock in my stomach.

The church at Window Rock, Arizona extended a call to me to serve as pastor of their church. Window Rock, 25 miles southwest of Tohatchi and just over the New Mexico-Arizona border, was home to the government offices of the Navajo Nation. My initial reaction was not one of great enthusiasm as I knew very little about the church. I was aware that it was a small congregation that was struggling with internal problems that were difficult to deal with. We knew that we had been under consideration by them for some time, but when the actual call came, I was not very excited about it.

By this time, we were nicely settled in again at Tohatchi and things were going well at the church. The relationship between us and the congregation was very good and we saw plenty of potential that challenged us. Our youngest son, Mark, had graduated from UNM and had accepted a teaching position at the Tohatchi High School and it was nice to have him close to us, although he did not live with us but rather in the staff housing at the school. There were good reasons for us to stay put, especially with things going well.

However, both Helen and I were aware that it would probably be good for us and for the church if we did take on a new charge before our eventual retirement would come. Helen was more enthused about Window Rock than I was. She was considering the advantage of serving a church where there were no boarding schools with children to teach and where our responsibilities would be lighter.

As we pondered over the call and talked it over and prayed about it more, the Lord did not give us peace with any intention to decline. The thought that came into my mind repeatedly was that to decline the call because of the problems in that church would not be right. After all, we had served on the mission field now for over 30 years and had run into problems in other places too. Still, the Lord had always been faithful and helped us through. Certainly the Lord would help us again if we depended on Him and on His power instead of our own.

Besides all this, we had gained plenty of experience in working out problems over the years. Having served on various committees of Classis Red Mesa had been helpful and had been good training for me. I had learned also from being a church visitor in Classis having to visit churches and sometimes having to help them through difficulties.

My thoughts ultimately went to Isaiah 6:8 where the prophet tells us, "Then I heard the voice of the Lord saying, 'Whom shall I send and who will go for us?'" We requested a meeting with the Window Rock council and also with the church members in order to become better informed about their church. This proved to be helpful to us and we accepted the call. We came to the agreement that we would move on March 4, 1995, the Lord willing.

Even though the congregation in Tohatchi was well aware of the call we had received, the news of our acceptance of the Window Rock position caused a stir. The church wisely decided to immediately call another pastor to take our place. During the few months before I left, I would give some helpful thoughts to them about what kind of pastor the church needed and the type of ministries the church wanted to give priority to.

We had time to get rid of a lot of the extra household items that had accumulated over the years. With our boys no longer living at home, the two of us did not need so much any more. We would also be moving into a parsonage at Window Rock that was much smaller than any other we had ever lived in, even though it was a rather normal-sized home by most standards and plenty big for us. Much of the extras were given away and there were plenty of eager takers. I also had to sell all my birds in the barn except for a dozen of my best pigeons for which I hoped to build a shelter in our next backyard.

The Tohatchi church sent us off with a farewell dinner and plenty of gifts of appreciation. The church would always remain

Chapter Four: Tohatchi

dear to us, having spent the longest portion of our married lives there, during which time we fell in love with the congregation and the community.

CHAPTER 5

Window Rock

A NEW LANDSCAPE

Window Rock, at a population of about 3,000, was easily the largest of the reservation towns we had worked in. The Neighboring towns of Ft. Defiance, St. Michaels, and Tse Bonito, the latter just across the state line in New Mexico, when added, gave the area a total population of around 8,000.

Moving Day to Window Rock was set for March 4, 1995, and when the day arrived, we were pretty much ready for it. For a few weeks, we had made a point of gathering cardboard boxes from Wal-Mart in Gallup and we had packed much of our belongings for the move. A group of men from the Window Rock Church came to move us. They brought with them some pickup trucks, a large flatbed, and a horse trailer. They also brought with them several tarps and other pieces of plastic with which to cover the furniture, as it was raining.

With an abundance of help, it did not take very long before the house was empty and all our worldly goods were loaded up and ready to go. We had previously agreed that the church men could do the moving instead of asking for professional help. This saved the church a lot of moving expense and it worked just as well.

The weather was not improving any as the day progressed. We had not only rain but even some occasional snow flurries and a very strong wind. It was hoped that everything would arrive at the new destination and that the covering would stay on during the 35-mile trip.

Helen and Buffie, our daughter-in-law, were the first to arrive at the Window rock parsonage where they washed cupboards, etc. By the time other vehicles arrived, Helen could tell the men where to

Chapter Five: Window Rock

put things. When I arrived, I noticed a huge number of vehicles as most of the church members had set aside the day to help with the moving. The new parsonage, considerably smaller than the one we had vacated, was crowded with people. The church ladies were in the kitchen to make a dinner for everyone while the others carried the furniture and boxes inside. Everything found a place somewhere in the house and was still in fine condition except for a few small items that had apparently blown off the flatbed unnoticed on the way, although that was of little concern to us.

We were pleased to see so many cheerful people help with the moving. Everyone was in an upbeat mood. This was evidence that they were looking forward to our coming and serving the Lord together with them. By the time everyone had left and we were alone, Helen was so tired that she had to sit down for a while and rest up. We then planned to return to the Tohatchi parsonage in a few days to clean it.

In our past homes on the reservation, as with most of the reservation churches, the parsonage was built on the main church property right alongside the church, but this parsonage was in the middle of a residential area known as the St. Michael's Housing. It was still only about one block from the church building, but we were going to be living right among many other neighbors to whom we would be reaching out with the good news of Jesus. The members of the church had the wisdom to purchase the parsonage a few years earlier as housing was very difficult to find anywhere in Window Rock. The church was proud to own a regular parsonage that could house a pastor family.

One of the first things we observed were the many dogs in the neighborhood. The rules in the books stated that a family could own no more than two dogs, but this rule was never enforced. One neighbor next to us had seven dogs and another had fifteen, while a third family owned three. The rules also stated that dogs were to be fenced in but this too was not enforced. We were thankful to have a good, strong fence around the yard to keep all those dogs out. We were well aware that packs of dogs could become a nuisance and even become dangerous, besides being a health threat. Cattle and horses also roamed around freely and they also could

Chapter Five: Window Rock

create problems in one's yard, as they were constantly in search for something to eat. There was no choice for us but to keep the gate closed all the time to keep all those animals out. Fences on the reservation, it seemed, were always meant to serve in keeping animals *out* of your property, not to keep them in.

We were blessed with a small lawn in our front yard, which was a rare thing on the reservation. Most people did not even try to grow a lawn in this dry country where water was scarce and where there were frequent dust storms in the spring. Fortunately, we were somewhat sheltered from the strong winds or else it would have been impossible to grow anything outside. At one time, the people made an attempt to grow a small lawn by the church building but that attempt soon failed when layers of sand blew in and covered the lawn completely. About the only thing one could do for landscaping was to plant a few small shrubs and then to keep them well watered. I brought some small and hardy lilac bushes from Tohatchi, where we had had many of them (many which I had transplanted myself) to grace my Window Rock yard. With regular watering, they would grow and do remarkably well, becoming the envy of the neighborhood.

The day after we moved in was Sunday and it had been planned that we would have an installation service at the Window Rock Church. Rev. Meekhof from Zuni, who had served as counselor for the church during the time of vacancy, was present to do my installation which was planned for the beginning of the service. When his part in the service was completed, he left to take care of the worship service in his own church in Zuni. I led the rest of the service and brought the message, followed by a potluck dinner.

AN IMMEDIATE CONCERN

A week after we moved into the Window Rock parsonage, most of our things were in place. We bought a few items such as drapes for the main windows and a carpet for the living room and for the bedroom. It felt better to have some covering over the cold tile floor. Then came up another matter that we had dreaded, one which would take all our attention.

It was a good thing that we had not had to rush to move out of

Chapter Five: Window Rock

our Tohatchi home as gradually Helen's heart condition had been getting worse. It had been thirty years since her first heart surgery in Utah, but now there were signs of recurring failure that would need to be corrected soon. These signs had come on gradually. Already, six years back in 1989, while on our way back from vacation, we had been forced to go to a hospital in Peru, Illinois when her heart was acting up. We were warned at that time of possibly more problems in the future. It became clear that after the move to Window Rock, Helen's heart condition would need our immediate attention. It would not be a pleasant matter to deal with and the timing of it seemed to be poor, but we had no other choice.

We had an appointment with the heart specialist in Albuquerque a week after we moved in. The doctors recommended surgery for Helen as soon as possible which was scheduled for a week later. We considered ourselves fortunate to be living no more that 165 miles from the nearest heart center where the dangerous surgery would have to take place.

On the way to the hospital, some of the same feelings and fears that we had experienced 30 years earlier in Utah came back to me again. There was no choice other than to go through with it and to leave it in the Lord's hands. So much had happened since the last time I had been faced with this, and God's faithfulness had continually seen me through it. The night before the surgery took place, I was in a motel room across the street from the hospital. It was pretty quiet in that room by myself, and I felt restless. I could not find peace until I reached the point where I was able to hand my wife completely over to the Lord, and said to the Lord, "No matter what Your will may be this time, I promise to continue to place my trust in you and to serve you whether you take my wife away from me or let me keep her." After this a wonderful peace came back over me and I was able to sleep so well that it almost made me feel guilty.

In the morning, I had to rush across the street to the hospital to say farewell to Helen before they took her away for surgery. When I arrived there, she was on the way to the surgery room but I was able to say a few loving words to her and show her my love. I felt proud of a wife who once again held such faith and confidence to face the surgery.

Chapter Five: Window Rock

The surgery was successful. Helen experienced a lot of pain, however, while in recovery. A week later, she was back home. The pain alleviated somewhat, but the recovery was slow. This was followed with a setback as she caught pneumonia and had to spend another week in the hospital in Gallup. This was a very difficult time. The coughing caused much pain, but she came through it as well and was able to return home again. Next, stomach problems developed which were caused by an ulcer and she was unable to keep in any food. This made her very weak and she had to be admitted to the hospital for another 1½ weeks. Finally, she returned home to stay. There was a gradual improvement, but she was weak and some of her problems would not go away. This led her to ask all our friends and relatives and our supporting churches to have prayer for her healing. The problems began to disappear.

Much of that summer, she also suffered from anxiety problems even though she was able to manage to take care of things in the house and participate at church. She never felt strong again that summer and we were beginning to wonder if the two of us would ever be able to do the work of ministry together again as we had done before. The anxiety problems left by the end of the summer and we were thankful that the heart surgery proved to have been a success.

These medical problems made it hard to get off on a good start in the new ministry. Between running back and forth to the hospitals and the doctors, I did my best to keep things going at the church, especially on Sundays. The congregation was very understanding and shared with us a lot of love and support during that first year. We appreciated their fervent prayers for us. We gained spiritual strength from it during this time which was hard on us, but also on them.

THE WINDOW ROCK CONGREGATION

The Window Rock Church was unique in that it was a younger congregation than the others we had served on the reservation. Window Rock residents were often people who had moved in from all over the reservation and left their places of birth to take up residence in a place where many of them had found employment.

Chapter Five: Window Rock

Normally, it was not common for people on the reservation to move far away from their families. Many were employed either by the Navajo government or by the Federal government's Bureau of Indian Affairs. This gave the church in Window Rock a better financial base than most other churches had on the reservation.

The tribal government was eager to employ the younger and the better educated members of its people. Many of the employees had leadership ability and had the tendency to be somewhat more aggressive than those out in "the sticks". On weekends and holidays, many of the people enjoyed visiting their parents and relatives in the area where they had been born. Although they were employed in the capital of the reservation, their hearts still remained in the open country and in their places of birth.

The church was blessed with some fine leadership and self-confidence. Moreover, there was a desire to be totally independent from outside financial support. Dependency upon denominational financial support was regarded as a necessary thing for a limited period of time but not indefinitely. The church was blessed with a capable treasurer able to do her job without the assistance needed in other churches we served.

In particular, the church was benefiting from leadership exerted by men such as Jack DeGroat who for years served as Regional Director for Home Missions for the Navajo churches. Jack, who was Navajo himself, was nonetheless familiar with church matters on a broader scale and understood the thinking of the mission board. Jack gave good advice and he and his wife Ellouise served as valuable leaders in the Window Rock church.

The name "DeGroat" came from one of our first missionaries to the Navajo. When his father started school, he needed to be registered with a last name, which the Navajo ordinarily did not have. It was decided to use the last name "DeGroat", and so he became a Navajo with a Dutch last name. Jack enjoyed telling the story of one of his first trips to Grand Rapids, Michigan to attend a Mission Board meeting where he ran into a problem. Arrangements had been made for him to be picked up at the airport. He waited for some time but nobody showed up for him. Finally, someone came up to him to ask if he happened to be Mr. DeGroat. They had been

Chapter Five: Window Rock

looking all over for him but were looking for a Dutchman instead of a Navajo.

As previously mentioned, this congregation had been dealing with some difficulties. During the 1960's, the church attracted many people and saw a lot of rapid growth. The congregation, however, drifted into questionable forms of worship. This caused some of the members to join other church groups while others attended no church at all. A small group remained, and this was the congregation we were asked to serve. The group was suffering from a lack of unity and some continued to hold to their questionable practices. Although these practices were not necessarily a bad thing, and the people did show a great amount of zeal for the Lord and were very sincere in their commitment to Christ, they were a divisive element in the church. Those who practiced these things had a goal of trying to win the whole congregation over to their point of view.

Some were teaching that when a person is sick, his sickness was caused by lack of prayer, lack of faith, or by some unconfessed sin. Others wanted the main emphasis of the church to be focused on miracles and healing, and less so on teaching and reaching the lost. We remained as tolerant as possible. Their charisma was appealing, but we were unable to accept their extremism and, so a lack of unity remained.

We dealt with this segment in the church with a lot of patience. After a few years, when it became clear that the rest of the congregation and the pastor were not inclined to join them, they eventually left the church. Some joined other groups or started their own church. The result was that there came a wonderful feeling of unity among those who were left. The people now became united in purpose and in prayer. New people soon began to show up and the church began to grow again as the people were involved in witnessing to others of their faith and inviting people to attend meetings at the church.

The members of the church were eager to participate in worship and serve as song leaders or share a short testimony of what the Lord had done for them. Faithful members took turns serving as leaders of the worship service using both the Navajo and English language. Stability in a service and some professionalism was

Chapter Five: Window Rock

appreciated. The message from God's Word was brought in English and without any interpretation into Navajo as this was not seen as a necessity here. The younger generation was more comfortable with English and much preferred the message delivered in it. We did a lot of singing in worship and it was still done in both languages. Even the youth and children enjoyed Navajo songs, especially when the school was beginning to teach classes in Navajo reading to the children.

After the morning worship service, people were encouraged to make use of a prayer room where they could share needs and have more prayer with a few of the leading church members. Almost every Sunday, people made use of this prayer room.

The word to best describe the Sunday evening services was "variety". Once a month, the whole church went to minister at a retirement home in Gallup. There we all sang together and we shared a short Bible message. On another Sunday evening, we all went to minister at the hospital in Ft. Defiance. We stood in the halls to sing to the patients. While we sang, a few of us would visit each room and talk with the patients and have prayer with them. This was a nice ministry but had to be discontinued when other churches wanted to do the same but were not careful about following hospital rules.

One evening per month, we also worshipped together with a few other churches in our area. The Bible Church in Tse Bonito and the Presbyterian Church of Ft. Defiance always got along well with us and we had wonderful praise services together. One Sunday evening each month we worshipped in our own sanctuary with a Bible lesson, singing, and prayer. If variety is truly the spice of life, then it worked well for us to have variety, as our people came out well for these second services on Sundays.

As in other congregations in the Reservation area, there was generally little concern for being prompt and on time. Often people joked about being on "Navajo Time", a vague zone somewhere between Mountain Time and whenever. The matter of coming to church meetings late was somewhat annoying to us at first, but by the time we were serving in Window Rock, we had become used to it and accepted it as a cultural matter. It was not unusual to have

Chapter Five: Window Rock

people come into church at the end of the sermon. Someone asked me one day, "Why is it that we have to go by the clock, especially on Sunday, which is supposed to be a 'day of rest'?" Still, most were on time.

Navajo Tribal Headquarters

Since Window Rock is the capital of the Navajo Nation, politics were part of everyday life and the church had to learn to keep politics from interfering in the life of the church. In some other churches, political matters sometimes brought hard feelings and, during election time, some of those who were running for office would try to intimidate the congregation to vote for them. I'm happy to say that this was not so in our church in Window Rock, and we were thankful for this. Our church did recognize those who were in government leadership positions and those who were employees of the Navajo government by holding a special service once a year where all the government people were invited. We shared some encouraging words from God's Word with them and had special prayer with those who asked for it.

Helen and I always enjoyed the friendly spirit in this church. We also admired their desire to learn and be taught from the

Scriptures. What was most impressive to us was that the strength of this congregation was in their prayers. There were some great prayer warriors in this church.

SURGERY ONCE MORE

Helen never felt strong the first year after her second heart surgery. The doctors watched her closely and soon realized that something was going wrong. The stitches that held the artificial heart valve in place were coming loose and we were told that there would be no choice but more surgery.

Helen's first reaction was, "I'd rather die than to have to go through all that again." Understandably, she was not prepared to go through so much suffering and misery a third time. After she had more time to think it over, she knew that for my sake and for the sake of the children, she had no option but to accept more surgery. We decided to make a special request to all our supporting churches, friends, and relatives that they pray for her and for a successful surgery. It was uncertain whether the artificial valve could be restitched or whether it needed to be replaced with a new one. The doctors were aware that the build up of scar tissue that resulted from the first two surgeries would make this surgery rather more difficult.

On the morning of the surgery in Albuquerque, sons David and Mark were there with me. Gordon Stuit, a fellow pastor who had served for years as pastor on the Navajo reservation, including at Window Rock, was also present. It was a six-hour surgery, and from time to time we were given an update on the progress over the telephone. Towards the end of the surgery, I received a call informing me that the doctors had run into a complication as they could not get the heart started up again. For one hour, we waited and prayed and then the welcome news came that all was well and Helen would be out of surgery soon. We sure had good reason to thank the Lord then.

The surgery turned out, in fact, to be a tremendous success. The doctors put in a larger heart valve. Helen had much less pain than she had experienced a year earlier and recovery went much faster.

Even in the midst of this trial, life had not been without some lighter moments. This time, the night after the operation,

Jim, who had arrived in Albuquerque by this point, and Mark stayed with me in the motel across the street, and I appreciated that. I was exhausted and fell asleep before they had a chance to sleep themselves, and my notoriously loud snoring they knew was destined to keep them awake. Not wanting to wake me up, they eventually decided to get up quietly and go out for a midnight breakfast. It was difficult for them to do all this in the dark so as to not wake me. In their stealth they only bothered to take one wallet, which was to be Jim's. They managed to get out without waking me up and enjoyed themselves at Village Inn for an hour. When it came time to pay, however, Jim reached for his wallet—and realized he had grabbed my billfold instead. They were grateful for my generous donation to their breakfast adventure and returned to the motel room (where a $20 bill was carefully replaced in my billfold in the morning).

When they came back, they found me still snoring as loudly as before. By 1:30, they still had not slept and began to talk softly. Eventually, I turned over and woke up, and on hearing them talking I told them, "If you don't quit talking, you won't get any sleep." I was sure wondering what I had said that made them stifle so much laughter.

After Helen and I returned home, there were some problems with fluid buildup in her chest which restricted her lungs from working properly, but that was all corrected. For one month, she had to be on oxygen, but recuperation continued. She became generally optimistic about life again and emotionally she became much stronger than before. The Lord was good to us. We felt blessed with so many people who had supported us in their prayers. Now the two of us could focus our attention on the church at Window Rock where we had come to minister for Jesus.

OPPOSITION

One of our church members was in great need of a job so that she as a single parent could provide for herself and her two children. She lost her job when her supervisor at work became angry and dismissed her for refusing to falsify certain records to make the department look better. This was a great temptation for her, but she

Chapter Five: Window Rock

chose to be without income rather than to join in sin. But the Lord rewarded her by providing her with another job even though jobs were very scarce and almost impossible to find.

Christians met a variety of opposition at the work place and often had to deal with discrimination because of their faith. Jack DeGroat was one of these. Other members of the church experienced more violent opposition. One young man was just beginning to show interest in the Lord and I had begun to instruct him and his wife with Bible teaching in their home. Not long after that, someone came to their house and aimed for his head and shot. The bullet grazed his head, and then went right through the wall of a neighbor's house and into the kitchen where it lodged in the microwave. This close call was certainly quite frightening for us. Again, this appeared to be further intimidation from the devil.

Another time, when one of our families went to take their turn as weekly church cleaners they were met at the church by two young men who asked them, "Do you love Jesus?" They answered with a clear "Yes, we do." They struck the man on the head with a steel pipe and ran off in the dark.

Graffiti on Window Rock Church Building

Chapter Five: Window Rock

The church in Window Rock as a whole went through a series of attacks aimed at the church building itself. Local gangs and satanic groups often came around the church. Time and time again, the outside walls of the church building were cluttered full of evil graffiti and foul language. The fence by the parsonage was also plastered with graffiti. It was apparently an attempt to intimidate us with fear and to cause us to suffer discouragement. The men of the church spent a lot of time repainting the church walls and the fence. It was somewhat discouraging that the Navajo police seemed unable to stop these hoodlums. Some people claimed that the police hesitated to do anything out of fear for their own lives, although it should be made clear that there was no proof to back up such claims.

One of these gangs broke into the church building and smeared paint on some of the pews and on the carpet. They identified themselves as "Insane Cobra Nation". They stole the amplifiers and even the aluminum offering plates. I was shocked to see the broken windows when I came to church early that Sunday morning. To my surprise, one of the church elders had come before me and was already cleaning up the mess. He said to me, "Pastor, don't feel so bad. See how they've written dirty words all over the carpet and on the doormat? That Devil is pretty stupid. Soon we will all be coming here for worship and we'll walk over the top of all that is written there and we'll be able to clean our dirty boots on it." In that worship service, I even made time for the entire congregation to go back to the church entrance and wipe their feet on what was written. In this way we showed our defiance of the Devil and his many helpers. Everyone got up out of their pews and was delighted to show their contempt for Satan by wiping their boots.

These break-ins went on for about a year. There were several smaller break-ins that did little damage other than broken windows. One day, when I went to church, I heard a noise inside. I unlocked the door and went inside and heard water running. The sinks in the kitchen and the janitor room had been plugged with the water turned on. Fortunately, the water was just running over the sinks when I arrived. No damage was done but there was a lot of water to be mopped up. Apparently the trespassers had been surprised by me

Chapter Five: Window Rock

and had left from the back door when they saw me coming.

One time, though, we successfully caught three people in the act. These were three young people who had broken a window and taken up residence in the church. They used the kitchen and cleaned out the food that was there. They had been sleeping in the back of the sanctuary and smoking dope. One of the mothers of the church and her three children surprised them when they came to clean the church building. They were headed for the broken window they had apparently come in through and were now frantically trying to escape. I expect they were quite surprised when the mother actually ran after them, bravely grabbing one of them as they tried to climb out. Eventually, all three managed to escape into the arroyo behind the church building and could no longer be seen. The police came quickly, however, and were able to track them down and catch them.

Slowly on, things improved. Our church struggled through this time, but the church was not destroyed. In fact, it grew in number and in strength. We hung two large signs high up on the outside of the church building. On the side that faced the highway, our sign said, "Jesus is Lord". The other sign above the parking lot said, "He is risen". This was a way the congregation could demonstrate to all to see that they were going to continue to share the gospel of Jesus, even if the enemy would stand in the way or might want to destroy them. We were not afraid of the public stand we were taking for Christ.

NEW MEMBERS

One Sunday morning, in the middle of the worship service, a mother and her young daughter came walking in and sat down on the very front pew. After the service, the mother explained that their family was going through hard times and were hoping to get some help. Later she told us that she and her daughter had gotten in the car that morning hopefully to attend a meeting at a church but they did not know where to go. They drove past some churches but chose not to stop. When they saw our church building with the sign "Jesus is Lord" on it, the daughter said to her mother, "That's the church where we have to go. It says 'Jesus is Lord' on it."

Soon we began to give her instruction in the Christian faith in her home. Her husband, who also claimed to have an interest, was holding back. His long and irregular work schedule and irregular sleeping hours were in the way of him participating in attending worship and in joining in the Bible instruction we gave to his wife. Then, for some time, we didn't see any of the family in church any more and she canceled her weekly Bible instruction with us.

One day, she called us by telephone to ask if we would continue our meetings with her. She began to attend church meetings again and her young daughter enjoyed Sunday school and committed her life to Jesus in her Sunday school class. The mother told us that her husband had promised that he would also attend church the following Sunday. Although we certainly hoped he would, we were having some doubts that he would actually do so.

A few days later, as I was coming home from Gallup, I saw the flashing lights of a police cruiser in my rear-view mirror and knew I'd been caught speeding. It can be an embarrassing thing to be a pastor and be seen pulled off of the road as I was then. The officer had already written out his ticket and was walking up to my vehicle. Surprised, he looked at me and said, "Oh, it's you!" It was the husband of the woman who had been attending recently. He said, "Pastor, I'm going to be in church this coming Sunday." He destroyed the ticket. I suppose embarrassment works both ways sometimes. He did attend church that following Sunday, and occasionally thereafter.

Some months later, the mother was baptized and joined the church. Her husband and three children were all there and sat by her in the front pew. She had decided not to wait any longer for her husband to join her. After the service, her husband walked up to me. "Pastor," he said, "I'm next." Some time later, he and the two older children were also baptized and joined the church. The family was eager to be of service and volunteered to help with getting the youth group started up again.

Fifteen miles north-northeast of Window Rock is the community of Navajo, New Mexico. Some years ago, this community attracted a lot of people. A large lumber mill employed around 250 people. The place was thriving and many new houses were built there. Our denomination began a new church there that

Chapter Five: Window Rock

had about forty worshippers on a Sunday morning.

The Environmental Protection Agency succeeded in shutting down the lumber mill claiming that the lumber industry was destroying the habitat of the endangered spotted owl. With all the jobs suddenly gone and no other employment available in that area, the community almost became a ghost town. The church was hurting also as members moved away in search of other employment. The church soon found itself unable to support a pastor or even a part-time pastor.

Home Bible Study in Window Rock.

Since the Window Rock church was the closest neighboring church, the people of Navajo asked me to help them by leading a Bible Study group one evening per week and a Sunday morning service once a month. With the consent of the Window Rock church, I helped out in Navajo for about one year. The work there was discouraging to me as the people were unwilling to give their personal support to the work except for one family. No matter how much I encouraged them, they did very little to invite others to come to the meetings. The attendance continued to drop. Eventually the work at Navajo was discontinued and the members were encouraged to join us at Window Rock or to attend other Christian churches in

Chapter Five: Window Rock

the area. The Mission Board discontinued its support and, probably, rightly so. In the end, one of the families of the Navajo church and two single men joined us in Window Rock. Sad as it was to see a congregation fold like that, we were glad to have the remainder as part of our small congregation.

The Vacation Bible School at Window Rock also brought in new families – four families and one single adult. After they received Bible instruction, they all joined the church membership. All remained faithful except for one family that left for another group. One little girl of about six came home from Vacation Bible School and asked her grandmother, "How come we don't go to church?" Her grandmother couldn't come up with a good enough answer and felt that the Lord was speaking through her grandchild reminding her to attend church as they used to do and to return to the Lord. When Helen and I came to their home as a follow-up on VBS, the family expressed a real desire to join us. They became a great asset to the congregation and still are today.

New people came into the church also through the witnessing that was done by our faithful members. They shared their testimonies with family and friends and co-workers and invited them to come. The church began to grow stronger even though growth seemed slow.

Two miles from us in Tse Bonito was a Bible Church with a small Christian School and a Christian radio station that broadcast the gospel message all across the reservation. We became good friends with the members of this church, and on Sunday evenings we worshipped together occasionally.

I was asked if I would be interested in teaching a few Bible courses on a college level to students from the surrounding area who had interest in these classes. For two years, I taught a class in church history and for one year a class on the life of Christ. I had a class of about eight students and they presented me with a real challenge, one I enjoyed very much.

One of the students in my class came by bike a distance of ten miles. He had recently been converted to Christ by listening to the Christian radio station. He had a great desire to learn and he would tell me again and again how the classes were a blessing to him. One

Chapter Five: Window Rock

day, he came to me and said, "I think I am in the wrong church." He had been attending a church which was known to be rather liberal in its teaching. He asked if he might visit the church where I was pastoring. The following Sunday, he was there together with his family. They never stopped coming and eventually he and his youngest son were received as full members in our church. His wife and another son are still struggling with making a full commitment to Jesus. His name is Joe and this is his story in his own words.

Hello,

My name is Joseph, or Joe. I am a Navajo and have four sisters and three brothers. I have lived most of my younger life and years of growing up in the upper part of northwest New Mexico near the Arizona border. I was brought up in traditional Navajo culture but attended meetings at a church with an Anglo background. My parents were participating in traditional cultural religious sings and events while also attending church services. We had to walk five miles to get on the church bus and this was followed with a ride of about seven miles to the church in Ft. Defiance, Arizona.

My father had an English Bible that he always read and then he told us Bible stories in the Navajo language. He had only five years of education at school, but he could read and write as if he were a high school graduate. This was a rarity for a person of his generation on the reservation in the nineteen-fifties. He did not attempt to teach us how to read. I guess that he never had the time to do so, or maybe he thought that school would take care of that. I never thought about God as a Father and Jesus as the Son of God. I did not think that deeply during my younger years. My thoughts were more on those wonderful white man's gifts that we received at Christmas time at our church.

Also I remember the parts of our life that brought suffering even in those days. The abuse of alcohol is an example. I used to hate the times when our parents went to the town of Gallup, New Mexico. They would come back very drunk and bring more alcohol with them. At times they would not come back for days and I had to assume the parent role around the age of seven or even younger and take care of my two younger brothers. During that time, my sisters were attending school in Phoenix and the older brother was in Salt Lake City, Utah.

Chapter Five: Window Rock

Father was a coal miner, rancher, farmer, and sheepherder. I learned early in life about taking care of livestock, to farm the field and to haul wood. My parents went to town once or twice a month to pick up a few supplies, but we lived pretty much on what we grew and raised ourselves.

When I first entered school at the age of six, I did not know any English except for "hello" and "good-bye" and a few other single words. But by the time I got to sixth grade, I could read way beyond my grade level. Besides the things boys of my age did, I read any book that was available at home. I remember receiving a big box of books from someone whose name I don't remember. By reading those books, I learned about different countries and lands beyond the Navajo reservation. I promised myself that someday I would go and see those places. I remember telling my mother that I wanted an oriental woman for a wife and did not want a Navajo.

I followed my dreams and left home for the first time at the age of twelve when I went to live at a government boarding school in Ft. Wingate, New Mexico. During the summer between eighth and ninth grade, a friend and I hopped on a bus and went to work irrigating the sugar beet fields in Oregon and Idaho. I loved that freedom and went back a few summers after that. After I completed high school, I left for good as I did not want to work for my father. I hated to work for him because I did not like my father as he was very harsh toward me and a hard man to please. He was very cruel when he punished me. I still carry a scar on the back of my head where he hit me with a piece of firewood.

I ended up in Los Angeles, California where I tried and did just about anything that I saw others do in those days of the nineteen seventies. I entered the military in California without telling my parents about it. When I asked to be sent to the eastern part of the country they sent me to Fort Knox in Kentucky.

Next I asked to be sent to Vietnam but by the time I got out of basic training and advanced training, the war was over. This was a disappointment to me and so I decided to request to be stationed somewhere overseas. The result was that I ended up serving in the Republic of South Korea. There, on a college campus in Inchon City, I met my first wife.

The military became my life. I loved the discipline, but also the opportunity for travel. All the countries I had dreamed about during

Chapter Five: Window Rock

my boyhood days I visited together with my wife and the two daughters we had. By the time I was twenty-five years old, my dreams seemed to be fulfilled. There was still an emptiness in me, however, and I thought that there must be more to life than I had discovered so far. I became disappointed with our lives and got into heavy drinking. Eventually, I was dismissed from the military and this ended my marriage.

It was during the early nineteen eighties when I and my two young daughters came back to the reservation. I got reacquainted with my family but continued to use alcohol. During that time, I became so miserable that I tried to end my life a couple of times. But both times I survived. I also was once robbed with a knife at my throat in Augusta, Georgia. Another time I was drunk and drove off a thirty foot cliff. This was the end for the pick-up truck but not for me. I spent three days in the hospital. I could have lost my life each time, but managed to get through these times. I gave myself the credit for this, but today I know differently. My Lord and Savior had a plan in mind for me. It was He who helped me.

My parents were beginning to be more involved in their church in those days and they influenced both of my young daughters. My older daughter asked me to go with them to church. I decided to go with them. The church was one that followed a lot of old customs and rituals and it taught some errors such as salvation by baptism and the holy Eucharist, but it nevertheless opened the door for me to come to my Father. I began to worship regularly and started to read my Bible.

During this time, my father would listen to the Christian radio station and I started to listen also. I started classes in a branch college. I was concerned about my daughters and the fact that I was a homeless man. I managed to get a full-time job and also became a full-time student, which was paid for under the old GI Bill. My mother was a wonderful help during this time and cared for my daughters when I was too busy to do so. I began to do more thinking about God and learned a lot by listening to the radio station. I became very active in the church where my parents were attending and thought that I was going to Heaven. But as I listened to the radio programs, I learned that I was not a re-born person. I was at first confused and started questioning my priest and some lay people but I was not getting the right answers back from them.

In 1985, I met my present wife while I was waiting for the bus to

Chapter Five: Window Rock

go to my classes. We started living together. I graduated from college in 1989; I was hired for one semester as a teacher and found out that teaching children did not suit me. I got a job at a hospital. We were married in 1991. During this time I continued to read the Bible and to listen to the radio programs, such as "Through the Bible" with Vernon McGee and "Unshackled".

In February 1999, while driving on the freeway to get to work, I was again listening to a radio program. The speaker was talking about "re-birth" or being "born again." He challenged his listeners by saying to them, "If you were to die in the next three minutes, do you know where you would be going?" I did not know the answer and it seemed like he was talking to me. I listened with full attention for I thought I might be going to hell. He talked about Romans 3:23, Romans 6:23 and Romans 10:9-11 where we are told, "If you confess with your mouth the Lord Jesus and believe in your heart that God has raised Him from the dead, you will be saved. For with the heart one believes unto righteousness, and with the mouth confession is made unto salvation. For the scripture says, 'Whoever believes on Him will not be put to shame.'" The speaker talked about the man in the New Testament who asked Jesus what it means to be "re-born" and being "a new person".

I started to cry and stopped my vehicle by the side of the freeway. The speaker on the radio asked his audience (including me) to follow his prayer word for word if they really wanted a new life and really meant it.

Incredible as it is, there I became a part of God's family. God's Word that had not always made sense to me in the past now was credible. I found meaning in those Bible stories that I had not seen or understood before. Psalm 110 says, "The Lord said to my Lord, 'Sit at my right hand till I make your enemies your footstool.'"

The church where I had been attending seemed suddenly cold to me. Every bit of free time I had I was listening and studying for I could not seem to get enough of reading and studying. My wife did not like the change in me. I know that I can never again be the same person that she married. Praise be to God Almighty who has made me find a Friend for ever. To this day, if I forget to read my Bible or to spend time in daily prayer, it will bother me until I do it. For me, my Bible, prayer, and running for exercise go hand in hand. I love to do each one each day.

Chapter Five: Window Rock

I went to my father and told him that I loved him and I asked for his forgiveness. My father lived to be 104 years old. A few days before he went to the Lord, I asked him if he was saved. He told me that as a young man he had given his life to Christ. He went to be with the Lord on April 11, 2002. I miss him, but I know that I will see him again. The faithful Bible reading he did in both Navajo and English is an example for me to follow.

I was so hungry for the Word of God that I was glad to learn that a Bible Study and other Bible courses were offered near the Christian radio station. I attended the classes and there met one of my teachers who would later become our pastor. He invited me to visit his church. My family eventually joined that church. I was taught to read my Bible and to study it in the Navajo language. Pastor and Helen K will always be close to our hearts. Even now after they have left this area, we still call them by telephone. They have led my wife and youngest son to the Lord. I am praying each day for the rest of my family and relatives that they also will ask Jesus into their lives.

It has been quite a ride for me on the Bible Bus, as Vernon McGee describes his life of living for Christ. One of my brothers is also following the Lord now and he led my mother to Christ. You know, Jesus is not just another holy man or a baby in a manger or a dying man on a cross. He is God, the Great Shepherd, the Cornerstone, our Kinsman Redeemer, our High Priest and He loves us all. So, whoever reads what I have written but does not have Jesus Christ as his personal Savior, I hope that that person will open his heart and let Jesus change his life even if you think that you have tried everything to get help. Jesus knows all about your problems and your sins. He is telling you, "Come to me all you who labor and are heavy laden, and I will give you rest. Take my yoke upon you and learn from me, for I am gentle and lowly in heart, and you will find rest for your souls. For my yoke is easy and my burden is light." (Matthew 11:28-30) These have become favorite Bible verses to me.

Go with Christ. Good-bye,
--Joe

DIFFERENT WORK

In the early years of my ministry, I used to spend a lot of my time making visits in the community and sharing the gospel in

Chapter Five: Window Rock

people's homes. This was true especially during the years we lived in Toadlena where people had more time on their hands and expected a missionary to come and make visits. This work declined drastically in Tohatchi where more people were employed and had better transportation, making them more mobile. In Window Rock, I did even less visiting in the community. Visiting with people had to be done in the evening when people were home but this was also the time for other meetings such as Bible lessons for new believers and meetings at church. The work of bringing the gospel to people was done more by the people in their daily contacts especially with co-workers at the place of employment. Helen and I made a point of visiting some older people in the daytime and we also visited the sick during the day. I had more time for lesson and sermon preparation, which was nice.

We did not do as much work with schoolchildren in Window Rock as we did in the other places. There was no government boarding school where we could teach Bible classes after school hours. We did hold a weekday Bible class for awhile for children who attended the Public school, but this had to be discontinued when they changed to four days of school per week and longer days. To be less busy was probably a blessing for us as our level of energy was no longer what it used to be. I even found the time to put together a family book with the history of my parents. This was done for the benefit of our children and grandchildren who would some day want to know more of their heritage.

In order to help people read the Bible in their native language and also to learn to read and sing songs in Navajo, I taught a weekly Navajo reading and writing class. This was an enjoyable class to teach each week and a highlight of the week. The people always appreciated our willingness to teach the reading of their language even though I knew very little Navajo and my pronunciation was far from being perfect. They also appreciated the fact that Helen was willing to be a student and learn along with them. It provided some humorous moments too, such as the time when someone held up a picture of a pig and asked in Navajo what it was and Helen volunteered to give the answer. Unfortunately, instead of saying, "It is a pig." It came out as, "I am a pig."

Chapter Five: Window Rock

I have asked one of the students from the Navajo reading class to share her story here:

Let me share some memories that I have of the Navajo reading classes in which I participated as a student.

When we first began our lessons, we started out each week by going over the vowel sounds, diphthongs, and the sounds of the consonants that are unique in the Navajo language. I still remember clearly that it was:

a as in Arthur
e as in Emma
i as in Indiana
o as in Ozzie

Slowly we proceeded to read words and then sentences. Also, we were given time to do dictation work and spelling. I could not get it at first and kept on writing the wrong strokes for high tones, nasal tones and glottal sounds. Even now, I still have a hard time hearing the nasal tones as I listen. This is probably because I speak it all the time without noticing these sounds.

We had a lot of fun learning from Pastor K. as our teacher. He had a lot of patience with us as we tried to read and write our own language. Today I am able to read pretty well the Navajo songs that we Christians sing. This is a blessing to me for I love to sing in Navajo as well as in English. To sing in my own language is wonderful and in my opinion we never seem to do enough of it at church.

Because of the kindness, love, and patience shown to us, we are now able to read our own language. I have now also joined the Evangelical Choir in our area. We sing mostly Navajo songs and I sing soprano.
  --Patricia Damon

It was decided together with the church counsel that attention would be given at church to four specific areas. These were:
- Improve the unity in the congregation.
- Work on having positive worship services with much participation from the members and with solid Bible preaching.

- Equip the members for better growth and service.
- Organize a stronger youth program.

To improve the feeling of unity, we made it a point to have regular fellowship dinners together at the church. These meetings did some good and were enjoyed by most. Usually, there was an abundance of food to eat for the people were very generous. Helen became famous for her delicious pork roast and scalloped potatoes. The church also went out on Sunday evenings to worship together at the hospital and at the retirement center in Gallup. These meetings were followed with a supper afterwards in a local restaurant. This, too, helped to create unity and the feeling of being a church family.

Our worship services were improved with the planning work done by a worship committee. Different families and individuals were scheduled to participate in the worship service and in the church program. The worship committee chose song leaders for each worship service, a worship leader, occasionally someone to give a short testimony of what Jesus had done in his life, greeters, church cleaners, nursery attendants, servers, etc. We even managed to organize a church choir and learned to sing with enthusiasm, although we never mastered singing in parts except for a few alto voices that harmonized with the melody. The music became an attraction and blessing to us. We had a good nursery which was also appreciated by people with young children and made for much less noise in the worship service.

Some teaching was given in small groups to equip members for better service and more spiritual growth. Lessons on stewardship were successful. Groups of three families plus some single members met together at the parsonage for three successive sessions. We learned about giving and tithing as taught in Scripture. In one of the sessions, each family or single member had to calculate amount of total income per year. From the total, they were then taught how to figure an amount as a tithe or other giving. Most of our people learned from this and the result of having these meetings was that the giving in church went up immediately by one third.

It was helpful to our Sunday school program to have an effective education committee. This committee worked on getting qualified

Chapter Five: Window Rock

teachers and suitable teaching materials. We were blessed with the help of one of the teachers at the local Christian school who was willing to serve as our Sunday school superintendent. By the time she reached retirement and returned to her home state of Minnesota, another member of the church took over as superintendent and served well.

Strengthening our youth program was the most difficult. The youth found it difficult to attend the meetings. They had to compete with a lot of after-school activities and the matter of transportation was sometimes a problem also. Several church members tried to work in the youth program but with minimal results. Helen and I tried also for a while, but also with minimal results. Although we had good rapport with them, they considered us as being "over the hill", as we knew we were.

We did our best, though, as we even joined the youth for a retreat up the mountain for two days and one night. We stayed in tents, with Helen and me using a tent that we had borrowed from some of our friends. To sleep in tents was no problem as long as everybody made sure to close up their tents well to keep the raccoons out. Some of the girls did not sleep well that whole night as a battalion of raccoons scavenged through our campsite and made all kinds of strange noises. Helen and I slept fine in spite of the noise. We were probably too tired not to be sleeping.

Helen and I had a couple nice breaks from our work in 1998 to attend the weddings of our youngest and oldest sons. Mark was married on July 25 of that year in Tacoma, Washington. We took a trip over there by car and had a great time. Jack was married on October 17 of the same year in Winston-Salem, North Carolina. With some savings that had been set aside for the occasion, all of us, except for the grandchildren, traveled together by airplane. It was enjoyable to be part of a Southern wedding celebration. Now each of our sons was married and we rejoiced that each was married to a Christian wife.

VOLUNTEER HELPERS

The church buildings needed our attention. The parsonage was in need of new roofing shingles, but the problem was that there was

Chapter Five: Window Rock

no money to pay for it. The Lord provided in an unexpected way. A couple came to visit the Window Rock church and they stayed with us at the parsonage. They noticed the need for new roofing materials and wrote out a check that would cover all the cost. The church men purchased all the needed materials and, within a couple of days, the roofing job was done.

The church building also had roofing problems. The strong winds that came every spring blew off several shingles each year. Although we did our best to keep them nailed down, there was always more damage done the following windy day. The building was in need of a new roof with solid plywood besides new shingles. This would cost a lot more money than what was spent on the parsonage repairs, but again we lacked the financial resources to fix the problem.

A youth group in Fenwick, Ontario heard about our problem. Their church was one of our supporting churches. The youth raised enough money to pay for a whole new church roof. They even offered to come and assist us with the work. We gratefully accepted their offer, but with the understanding that they would not do all the work for us, but rather assist us and work under the supervision of our church men. The Fenwick group even brought a few men who were familiar with carpentry work and had the necessary tools to work with.

In a few days, the job was completed. One day, I counted as many as 27 workers on the church roof, all of them working together beautifully. Most of the work was done in the evening after five o'clock when our church men returned from their jobs and were able to help them. By the time it became dark, several of the church families arrived to put on a meal for everyone.

The girls of the Fenwick group all stayed with families in the church. The boys stayed in a house trailer on the side of the mountain ridge. We had had some rain showers that summer and there were even some mosquitoes, normally rare in this area of the trailer house. The owner of the trailer house, however, taught the Ontarioans a traditional way of keeping away the mosquitoes. He made a few small piles of dry horse manure around the trailer and set the manure on fire. To the delight of the boys, this certainly took

Chapter Five: Window Rock

care of the problem.

The following summer, three married couples from another supporting church in Listowel, Ontario volunteered to assist us with painting both the outside and inside of the church building. Again, we made it clear that we would gladly have them assist us in this big project but that our church men would supervise the work. These volunteers and our church people worked together beautifully and in one week of work the job was completely finished. Again, in the evening, we had our meals provided and enjoyed each others' fellowship.

A youth group from the Imlay City, Michigan church indicated a desire to visit for a week and to help out wherever we could use them. We asked them to serve as assistants in our Vacation Bible School but explained that we wanted our own people to do the teaching. We asked them to hold meetings and a spiritual retreat with our church youth. This, too, worked out well. Again, the same house trailer was used as the previous year to house the boys and their leader and his wife. It was agreed that they would prepare their own breakfast in the trailer each morning. The first morning the youth leader and his wife took it upon themselves to purchase a few groceries for their breakfast. Communities on the reservation are not generally laid out in an organized fashion with named streets such as they are in most places in the U.S. On the way back from the grocery store, they were unable to find their trailer and got lost. After driving around for some time, they finally came to ask for directions from us. They hesitated to admit that they were lost in such a rural area but learned a lesson in humility, one which most of us thought was rather funny. To have to live in the open country was a good experience for these young people from the east and they enjoyed it.

Yet a fifth group of volunteers helped out with Vacation Bible School and came to socialize with our church youth. This group was again from Listowel, Ontario where the church painters had come from a few years earlier. They also worked out well.

Of course, we in Window Rock benefited from all this help, but I believe that the visitors gained even more from having a cross-cultural experience in a mission setting.

Chapter Five: Window Rock

PREPARING FOR THE YEARS AHEAD

The time we spent at Window Rock seemed to go by very fast. This was probably due to the fact that we enjoyed being there so much. It was a joy to work with a congregation that was so responsive and willing to learn. Their desire to become more responsible Christians challenged us.

The time came near for our anticipated years of retirement. The church had some big decisions to make to prepare for potential difficulties ahead. The church council therefore took some time to study the church and to set some goals for the years ahead. You cannot really call a new pastor without knowing your church program and knowing what kind of pastor you need. The responsibility of choosing pastors and of providing for them was something that used to be the responsibility of the Mission Board together with the input from the vacant church. Now that some of the churches had matured into organized churches, this responsibility was first with the church, and rightly so. This was something that was new to the church and needed careful study. We also needed to look into the church's ability to provide for a pastor financially. The church needed to decide whether it would be served best by a Navajo pastor or whether an Anglo would be able to function adequately, even when he might be unfamiliar with the culture and the people in our area.

The council studied some of the procedures normally followed in calling a new pastor. They put together a job description for a pastor at Window Rock and put together a proposed financial package. It became abundantly clear that not every pastor would be suitable to serve in this church. He would have to be able and willing to live on a lower salary compared to that in other parts of the country and he and his family would have to be able to adapt to a different cultural situation.

During our last year at Window Rock, the congregation already began to work on getting in contact with potential candidates. The denominational headquarters was very helpful and provided the church with a list of pastors who had indicated an interest in possibly serving in this part of the country and in a cross-cultural situation. Helen and I made a point of staying away from giving

Chapter Five: Window Rock

our personal input on calling a new pastor. This was a matter for the congregation to deal with. We gave some information and supported the people with our prayers.

Helen and I also had to do some important planning for our own future. We had always thought of living out our retirement years somewhere close to the reservation such as in Gallup or Farmington. Reservation law, which required non-natives to be working on the reservation in order to live there, did not permit us to remain on the reservation past our retirement years, but we were hoping to be able to live in the area close enough to be able to help out in various Navajo churches where they might need temporary help. We had noticed, however, that both of us always felt better physically at a lower altitude. Most of the reservation area was well over a mile high in elevation. Helen was able to take longer walks in the lower altitude without getting overly tired. I, myself, felt better too, especially in a climate that was more humid. For years, the dry climate of the Southwest caused a bad rash for me every winter along with severe itching. We, therefore, came to the conclusion that perhaps it was best for us to leave this area of the country. We settled on moving to Michigan where we would be close to our siblings, even though we would be far away from our children. The chance of ever living close to our children was pretty small. David and Jim were well settled in New Mexico with its high altitude while Jack was living in North Carolina in the east and Mark in Washington State in the west.

We set our sights on Michigan, in Helen's hometown of Imlay City. One of her brothers had continued living there along with two married nephews and a married niece. We also were attracted to the Imlay City Christian Reformed Church, which had been one of our faithful supporting churches for about 30 years. Most of my own siblings lived across the border in Ontario and Helen's were in Michigan except for one. One other important thing was that, in Imlay City, we would be quite close to an airport from where we could easily and quickly fly to any part of the country whenever we wanted to make a visit to our children.

The Imlay City church welcomed the idea of us moving into their area. One of the church elders who was about to sell his house

Chapter Five: Window Rock

called us to let us know that he had his house for sale and he would be happy to sell it to us. The house was just the perfect house for us and in a perfect location. We ended up buying it—the first home we had ever bought. We were well aware that it would be a big adjustment for us to assimilate ourselves again to eastern life and to take part in church activities, but the Lord would provide us with new challenges and new opportunities to serve Him there.

The final two months at Window Rock was a time of special gatherings, farewell meetings, and, of course, the preparation for the move itself. The moving date was set for August 26, 2002. During July, one of the Tohatchi families honored us with a mutton roast at their summer camp high on the mountain. This was truly a wonderful time of sharing the things the Lord had done over the years. And a meal of roasted mutton and fried bread and fresh coffee is hard to beat.

A month before was our 40th wedding anniversary on August 3. Our children arranged for a three-day retreat at a camp high in the mountains. All of our children and grandchildren were there with us for three fun-filled days. Even my youngest brother Bill and his wife Mary, plus two of their daughters and a son-in-law joined us. They were on their way to Phoenix from Canada for my nephew's wedding and it worked out perfectly for them to join us for the happy occasion.

The Window Rock church organized a camp-out with us on the mountain by Assayi Lake. This is a beautiful area where over the years I spent a lot of my free time fishing. The people put together a program of activities that included a time of fishing together. We also went on a nature walk and enjoyed great fellowship and worship time together. The evening was spent around a campfire where we shared our feelings about leaving the mission field and gave thanks to God for our time there. As for our attempt at fishing, a few people were fortunate to catch a few.

The church also organized a final farewell meeting for us and all the area CRC's to be held on the Rehoboth School campus where they had enough room. Christians from various churches were invited to share, especially those from the former churches we had served. The people put on a great dinner with much delicious

185

Chapter Five: Window Rock

food. There was a beautiful farewell program in our honor. The large meeting center was full of people. To our surprise, the vice-president of the Navajo Nation, Dr. Taylor McKenzie and his wife Betty were also present. This couple is special to us as they are the parents of our daughter-in-law, Claire. Also the Speaker of the House of the Navajo Council was present. They presented us with a special plaque to show appreciation for having served as missionaries among their people for 39 years. This was an honor for which we were not prepared. The Mission Board, with whom we had served for all those years, also honored us and had a representative present. Classis Red Mesa, which represented all our Navajo churches also honored us and shared words of appreciation. The people showered us with gifts that evening as they said their farewells. A lot of tears were flowing, including ours. It was very moving to listen to a farewell speech from our oldest grandchild, Stephanie, and a beautiful solo from our little grandson Joshua, who sang loud and clear "Jesus Loves Me".

Early in the morning on moving day, five church families took time to say a special final goodbye. The love that was shared with us in such abundance is something that we will never forget. Although we were moving to Michigan, it was obvious to us that part of us would remain with these precious brothers and sisters in Christ.

The following morning we set out from Gallup to head east across the plains and back to where we had come from 39 years earlier. Things were different after these years in which the Lord had guided us in ways and through circumstances that we could never have anticipated. With the help of our son, David, to drive one of our vehicles, we headed into the next chapter of our lives.

Conclusion

The Christian Church on the Navajo Reservation has entered a new era. The years of sending "white" missionaries to bring the gospel of Jesus from camp to camp are past. Many of the Navajo people have heard the gospel message and the Lord is building His church all across the reservation. What was begun about a century ago must now be carried on today primarily by the Navajo Christians themselves. They have been given a big challenge as 90% of their people still do not consider themselves as Christians and are still without salvation. This work will be carried on successfully if it is done in the power and spirit of Jesus in whom "all things are possible." (Mark 10:27).

One thing about the Navajo people that always impressed me is their high level of spirituality. It is much higher than what we find among the average American population, including my own relatives and friends. Matters such as prayer, worship, funerals, weddings and dreams and visions are seen as very important and therefore received a great deal of respect. Even in the Navajo government, which is not known as a Christian government, daily meetings are often opened with prayer and this, apparently, without objection. In my visitation with people, I usually suggested that we pray before I left. This was always well received regardless of whether we all believed in a Christian God or not.

Even children in the boarding schools would ask for prayer when they had special concerns. When Helen was substitute teaching and eating her lunch in the school cafeteria, some of the students noticed that she took time for prayer before she ate her food. Some of the students then asked her if she would pray with them too. These students had grown up with a respect for spiritual things. In one of my Bible classes with the students, I taught about Satan and how it is his aim to destroy us and everything that is loved by God. Some of the students in the class raised their hands and asked me if I would pray with all of them for God's protection from the Evil One. It is hard to imagine such a response, albeit an appropriate one, coming out of mainstream America today.

Also, the existence of God is not an issue with the Navajo as it is with many other people today. I have never met a Navajo who claimed that he was an atheist. They know that there is a Higher Being and a Creator of all things. From the keen observance of the things around them, they are aware that Someone has created all this and that He must be wise and powerful and One who loves beauty and order (Romans 1:20). This is why they are taught in their traditions that they must "walk in beauty". In their desire to reach out to God and to worship Him, however, they worshipped His creation instead of God Himself, as is common to many people in the world who do not know God, having been blinded by sin from knowing the truth. Unless that particular blindness is removed, they will never know the full truth about God and His wonderful salvation for sinners.

We have often been asked by people why we spent so many years with the Navajo and telling them to come to faith in Christ when they are already so religious. It is true that they have always been a very religious people, but it must be made clear that to be religious is not the same as being a Christian. Without knowledge of the Savior and of God's salvation for sinners, people are still lost. They are without hope and live with constant fear. This is why people specifically need the Bible preached and taught to them and why they must learn to read the Bible.

Sometimes when people express their objection to the Christian faith, it is not so much an objection to teaching God's plan of salvation through the death of Jesus on the cross. Their objection is with teaching that Jesus is Lord of our life as well as our Savior and He must therefore be obeyed. We must put aside all that is evil or that dishonors the Lord. This is what is often seen as being anti-cultural and anti-social and therefore as something undesirable.

Thank God that His truth has also reached the Navajo. The veil of darkness that caused them to worship in ignorance is steadily being removed. Now that the truth has come to them, the Lord is also calling them to repent and turn to Jesus for their salvation (Acts 17:29-30).

Satan, the enemy, does not appreciate those who bring the

truth of God and we know that he will therefore do all he can to stop such people. This is why the mission field is a battleground. Those involved in the work of missions, including the new Christian people, find themselves in the front line of battle. This is why we must never forget the churches in this as they need prayer support, just as they have faithfully prayed themselves all these years.

When we observe the Navajo churches, we should first take note of its strengths. One will soon conclude that these churches certainly are not like helpless little infants that are struggling seemingly forever to mature while stumbling and bungling along the way, though one might quickly come to that conclusion. One of these strengths, then, is their commitment to prayer as its importance is instilled deep within them. They believe in spending time in both private and public prayer. Even young children are often willing to lead in a prayer for this has been taught to them at a young age. Not only do the people pray, but they have a strong faith that God will answer a Christian's prayer. Answers to prayer are readily shared with one another, as are also prayer concerns.

In the Navajo churches, there is a great deal of compassion for one another especially during times of need or sickness or grief. Relationships are of great value to them. As burdens and cares are shared with each other, there is always a time for prayer for one another. The people do not hesitate to express their emotions and openly display their love for the Lord and for each other. They have a keen understanding of the fact that the Christian faith affects every aspect of our daily life.

The worship services can be very enjoyable and are positive as long as the churches are allowed the freedom to worship in their own cultural setting. An informal style of worship is preferred to one that is strictly enforced without any room for alterations. Usually a great deal of time is given to singing and prayer in a worship service.

The Christian Reformed Churches on Navajoland are blessed with a system of government that was introduced in the churches over the years, but has been revised to make it suitable in this culture. This has helped to keep the churches stronger compared to many other small church groups on the reservation. The Christian

Conclusion

Reformed churches hold themselves accountable to God, but also to each other as they stand united in their goal of helping to build God's kingdom. In contrast, the majority of the native churches are independent little house churches that minister basically to one or two particular clans and are controlled and led by a lay pastor.

But, as in all churches, the Navajo churches have their areas of need also. The lack of native pastors has been a concern for many years and still is a concern today. There is a need for native men and women who are willing to make a total dedication and a sacrificial dedication of themselves in the area of ministry. They need to feel a divine calling into the ministry rather than to look at it as a low paying job compared to other professional work. The churches also need encouragement. They are suffering discrimination for having left traditional religious ways. Christianity is wrongly viewed in their neighborhoods as being anti-cultural and anti-social.

The churches on Navajoland also have a need for more acknowledgment as part of the church at large. Too often they are still thought of as being immature and as churches-in-embryo. This has a negative effect just as it would to a young man who is constantly told that he is immature and cannot do many things right. The church at large needs to be open to learning from their native brothers and sisters in Christ who have many spiritual riches to share. Many local congregations were hurt by an attitude brought upon them by the denomination in general, as well as from the white missionaries it sent to work on the reservations, that they were in constant need of "parental" supervision. Certainly some missions were younger and more immature in the faith and needed the heavy guidance and support, but it often felt as if they were not allowed to grow, or at least to grow in a way which fit their needs as they themselves perceived it, not as viewed from Michigan. So often, churches on the reservation were so continuously sheltered from the responsibility of flying on their own, that they never seemed to truly learn to fly at all. This attitude of paternalism in which we had been working for many years was unhealthy and created continuous dependency.

Alcohol has caused much suffering among our native people and brought much dysfunctionalism in their society. The results of this are felt in the churches also and the churches have to learn to deal with these difficult matters. While these problems are very real, we may never make the mistake of thinking that all native people are alcoholics and dysfunctional. This assumption is the case in much of America today and it is painful to the Native American Christians and an untrue picture of them. Activities such as smoking or drinking are considered by them as belonging to this sinful world that must be put aside. The idea of social drinking is not understood by most because on the reservation one drinks only for the purpose of getting drunk.

The question is sometimes asked how help and encouragement can be given to the Navajo churches. I will share a few thoughts on this that may be helpful.

An off-reservation church can investigate the possibility of becoming a "big sister" church to a small native congregation. This would ensure communication about prayer needs and financial needs or needs for teaching materials. For example, left over VBS and Sunday school materials can sometimes be very useful. At the same time, they could send the native church some of their own prayer needs so they can support each other in prayer.

Navajo Scenery

Epilogue

Perhaps the two congregations could schedule some visiting between each other in order to share spiritual experiences and to gain an appreciation for cultural differences. While visiting a church on Navajoland, they could see how the Lord has been building His kingdom in that area. They may also be able to explore some of the unique beauty of the Southwest such as seen at the Grand Canyon, Arches National Monument, Canyon De Chelly, and many other places.

Individual Christians or families can become prayer supporters and make friends with a congregation or a certain family that may be interested in a special relationship. Regardless of what one might do, in each of the above, one should be careful not to have an attitude of paternalism.

Finally, I believe that a fine way of serving the Navajo churches lies in the area of education. Dedicated Christian teachers are needed in Christian Schools, Public Schools and Government Boarding schools on the reservation. The latter two have not been fully explored as opportunities for bringing the Christian faith in this area, but I believe that they hold great potential. Most teachers would probably prefer to be working in a Public School rather than a school run directly by the federal government. Housing is usually provided on the school grounds at a reasonable cost to the teacher. The teacher can affiliate with one of the local Christian churches and eventually offer to help as a Sunday school teacher if needed or possibly as a youth leader. Almost all churches are looking for help in these areas. Even though the teacher may not be permitted to teach Christ in the classroom, there are plenty of opportunities to do so after school hours. This is a good opportunity to represent Christ among the Navajo people and to encourage the believers today.

Epilogue

Now in the year 2007, we make our permanent residence in our home at 268 Engle Street in Imlay City, Michigan. Since the day we left the reservation to take up residence in Michigan, Helen and I have done interim pastoring for 4 months in Volga, South Dakota over this past winter. Previously we had returned to the reservation for two winters to serve as interim pastor in two of the churches that were without a pastor. We were in Window Rock for two months during the winter of 2004 and at Tohatchi in 2005. It was an especially rewarding experience to be back in those places. The best thing for us was to see that the church of Jesus continues to be there and it is there to stay. Jesus, the King and the Builder and Provider of His Church, will keep it in spite of the many struggles and obstacles it must cross. The Good Shepherd who loves His sheep and knows them will never leave them nor forsake them. We may not forget them, as they deserve and need our love and support.

Helen and I are as busy today as we want to be and are finding plenty of opportunities to serve the Lord. We are working mostly with the elderly and shut-ins. We are also in charge of leading a weekday time of worship at a retirement center. Helen still teaches children and she loves to read. She is an avid Scrabble player. I love my vegetable garden and yard and, of course, still love to go fishing as much as I always have. On occasion, I still preach and enjoy doing it. Both of us enjoy hosting guests at our home.

Our son Jack and his wife, Jodie, have recently moved from North Carolina to the Southwest. They are now living in Durango, Colorado where Jack writes devotionals for Tyndale House Publishing, as well as doing other work. Jodie used to work in Marketing and Administration for a non-profit organization, but is now keeping busy as a stay-at-home mom for their two children Will and Anna. They are serving the Lord faithfully, always open for new ways to be involved in building God's kingdom.

David and his wife, Claire, and the children Peter and Grace are living in Grants, New Mexico. David is employed by the State

Epilogue

as County Director of Human Services. Claire is occupied with homeschooling their children. They all love the Lord and are eager to take on opportunities for ministry in God's kingdom. Claire is a math teacher by profession and will probably continue working after homeschooling is done.

Jim and his wife, Buffie, are residing in Gallup, New Mexico where both are teaching in the public school system. Jim teaches US history while Buffie teaches Home Economics. They have three beautiful children –Stephanie, Andrew and Joshua. Jim is active in the Gideons and often is asked to speak at Navajo churches in the area as a Gideon representative.

Mark and Sharon are living in Tacoma, Washington. Mark is teaching English and Geography at Federal Way Public Academy, a college preparatory middle/high school. Sharon is also a teacher, but is presently proud to be a stay-at-home mom to their daughter, Rebecca. They are active in a large church where Mark enjoys being part of the drama team helping to reach the lost.

Our many thanks go out for the wonderful support we have received over the years from the Christian Reformed Church Home Mission Board, our many supporters, and the Navajo Christians. We will always remember their loving embrace. This book was written in appreciation of them all.

Printed in the United States
104588LV00001B/313-408/A